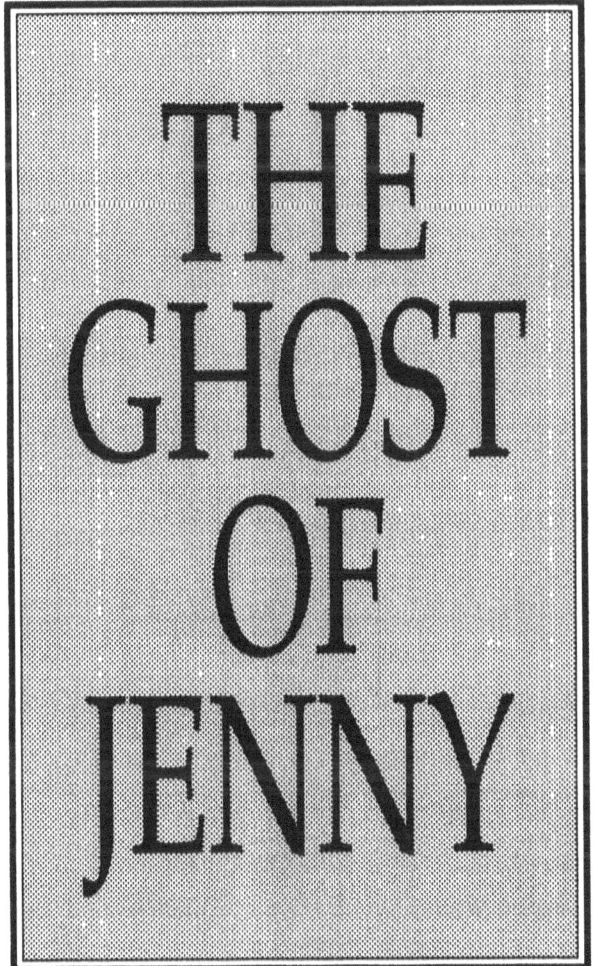

MARY JOE CLENDENIN

Author of GONZALO: CORONADO'S SHEPHERD BOY

toExcel

San Jose New York Lincoln Shanghai

For Ray

with all my love

INTRODUCTION

E very day we are asked to accept many astonishing discoveries and creations: nuclear fusion, holograms, supersonic speeds, laser surgery, gene alterations, and computer communications so swift they are almost instantaneous. Some developments are indeed so fantastic our minds protest against their credibility—to the point where we finally hear ourselves saying, "I find that hard to believe."

Some readers will look on the story of a ghost as just another myth or legend designed to trap the unwary, a test of one's gullibility, of no more substance than science fiction that imagines full blown civilizations in the next-nearest galaxy. While they use technology their grandparents could never have imagined, they steadfastly hold out against anything that cannot be proven scientifically. In the present world of shocking reality, I find no reason not to believe some of the ghost stories experienced by people I have known.

My father, Joe E. Fitzgerald, a nurseryman of Erath County, told me many of these stories from the time I was old enough to listen. To him the ghost of Jenny was very real, or at least the stories told by those who encountered her were real. He wrote stories about ghost sightings for the local newspaper and did his part to keep the legend alive. As a young man, he received a letter from Jenny's husband after he fled to Oklahoma Territory to escape a lynching party. That lynching, in which the last man on the limb (not necessarily named Papworth) was rescued, is one of the facts of the legend. My dad also knew the man who murdered Jenny, and may have preyed on the culprit's conscience when he wrote a letter to the paper and signed it, "The Ghost of Jenny."

Sounds vibrate on the airways that human ears are incapable of hearing without instruments. Light waves we cannot see exist both above and below the visible spectrum. Perhaps spirits are like these invisible and inaudible light rays and sound waves. Right now, half a dozen gibbering spirits may be watching over my shoulder as I write, and need only the special instrument of imagination to be seen and heard.

I claim no special knowledge or experience of my own, just an active imagination to fill in some of the blanks that revolve around the McDow Ghost Hole, and look into a world of possibilities. So, using often-told tales, I've woven my own story around them. I don't ask you to believe, just to enjoy.

"From the most ancient days, men have not merely
believed in ghosts; they claim to have seen them,
heard them, and even to have touched them "
—HERBERT A WISE
Great Tales of Terror and the Supernatural

CHAPTER I

The First Appearances

It was that fraction of the hour before the sun came up, when night critters were taking a last sniff around their territories and daylight creatures were beginning to yawn and begin their daily chatter. The general transition at McDow's watering hole on Green's Creek was interrupted by the thumping of a tired horse bearing an equally tired rider. The rider, with frowzy brown beard, impatiently let the horse make its own trail, scattering gravel as it went thirstily to the water. The man had been riding hard to get back to home territory after his participation in the dark deeds that took place several miles westward. As he swung a leg over to dismount, his spur caught the material of a black hood partially sticking out of his saddle bag. He turned to loosen his foot, then stood transfixed, startled by a hissing noise.

Directly in front of the horse, the surface of the water bubbled and boiled, in a barrel-hoop-sized area. He cringed as with a burst of fury something—some unspeakable something swaddled in vapor—burst through the surface of the water and rose to tower over him. His fidgety eyes, for once focused, bulged as the vapor quickly dissipated to reveal a horrible apparition swaying above the water. With a skeletal face lit by eyes of fire and matted hair that stood weightless out from the skull, the spectre materialized. As she reached toward him with long bony fingers, he was assailed by a putrid overpowering smell that robbed him of breath. The horse bolted, no longer thirsty. Rolling its eyes, it raced back up the bank with the man clinging like a cocklebur to mane and saddlehorn. A piercing scream, ending in wicked, joyless laughter, followed the rider as it echoed along the creek bank.

The ghost of Jenny was utterly and painfully confused. What was her purpose? Why was her spirit tormented? What must she do to find peace? How long must she wander with such a sense of utter abandonment? How long did ghosts need to become accustomed to life without a physical body, to learn to cope with an existence dominated by uncontrolled emotions? Not having been a ghost very long, Jenny didn't yet know the rules that governed a ghostly existence. She was still experimenting with her newly found power and sensitivity. The ability to be a part of life as it once was and, at the same time, to be a spectator, added a dimension to existence that was revealing, yet painful beyond imagination. Confused by new limits of existence, her anger grew and fueled the consuming rage and resentment that caused her denial of a restful death. Had there been eyes able to behold the actual transformation from living woman to wandering ghost they would have seen the storms of hate, envy and resentment that exploded in all directions and then were drawn back together by the magnet of her soul. All she knew, since it was happening to her and not another, was that she had been sentenced to wander, to haunt until—until—she knew not when.

Most people, if they think of ghosts at all, think of some horrible manifestation that is in complete control of events and locations. They have little sympathy for the ghost itself. Imagination is used up in the beholding, not in empathy. People go through life focused on perception of themselves, their feelings, hurts, frustrations, joys and disappointments only as they themselves are involved. Some brave souls, poets, some grandparents, and foolish ones who think they can walk in others' shoes risk empathetic heartbreaks. Most are wrapped in small bundles of ego. Only one, the Christ, knew the secret thoughts and motives of others, and he died of a broken heart.

Remembering herself as a small woman, with beautiful auburn hair and a flashing smile that showed slightly crooked teeth, a disfigurement too slight to truly mar her beauty, Jenny wondered how she looked now. Though she was conscious of every imperfection, imagined and real, while she lived, she had no way of knowing how horrible she looked as a ghost. Never having seen her ghostly image, nor would she ever be able to do so, she found it difficult to accept the awe and sheer terror she created in those to whom she appeared. Her horrible matted hair, gaunt face with burning eyes, and ghostly form which now appeared to others were not reflections of physical features, but of raw, ugly emotions.

The ghost of Jenny clutched the spirit of the baby to her, knowing intuitively that the comfort it gave would not be with her long. She had loved her baby beyond her own expectations, and had been a loving, nervous mother attending needs at first hints of discomfort. Because of the way the baby had died, being slung against the cabin wall and murdered as Jenny fought and screamed for the lives of both herself and the baby, the innocent spirit of the baby was with her. Somehow, Jenny knew that the purpose of the baby's sojourn in the world of restless spirits was to torment the guilty. Though she didn't know for many moons why she was sentenced to haunt the living, Jenny knew the reason was not the same as her child's. Clutching the baby girl to her, Jenny crooned, but the singing turned into eerie echoes among the trees along the creek bank.

The ghost of Jenny was haunted. She was condemned to, not just remember, but relive, painful scenes from her life over and over again, as she wandered, searching for she knew not what. When burdens of memory came upon her, she was compelled to be both audience and actress as scenes from the past unfolded. In the scenes she saw things that escaped the living. Longings of the heart and unexpressed feelings wracked her being. Misery and discontent allowed her no rest. Though she had discovered her physical boundaries to be the vicinity of their cabin which her husband Charlie Papworth and good neighbors had built near Green's Creek one day in 1880, scenes of her life ranged over all of its thirty years.

"Oh, please! Not that one again," she begged of whatever force was in control of both the living and the living dead. But she knew her pleading was for naught as her phantom hovered over a clear hole of water in the creek and she began to relive a horrible day of the move from Georgia to Texas.

With despair in her heart and a hopeless look on her face, Jenny, in her mud splattered and begrimed long skirts and bonnet, took her place behind the covered wagon. The road was a faint trail where the brush had been thinned and which the hard rain last night had changed to a quagmire. Charlie was at the heads of two oxen, Maud and Missy, patiently coaxing and helping them pull. As a back wheel dropped into a hole, the team abruptly stopped.

Charlie yelled, "Come up here and lead, Jenny. Let me get back there and push."

Her heart full of resentment and anger at the commanding tone in his voice, Jenny silently refused to obey orders again. She muttered to herself as she lifted her muddy skirts, put her back to the wagon and pushed with all her might.

"Just listen to the sweet words he says to those oxen and then how he talks to me. Sounds like the sweet talk he used when I was all dressed up in the courting days. Now he talks kinder to his animals."

Her ghost pleaded as she watched, *"Just hear the love. It's there. You are both so tired..."*

As she held and tried to lift the wagon bed, the rough boards bit into her once soft white hands, now calloused and chapped, but her slight frame added little to the efforts of the beasts. Her once pretty shoes slipped and slopped and felt like they weighed tons with the clinging mud gluing them to the ground.

Muttering under his breath at the obstinacy of his wife, Charlie pulled on the yoke and encouraged the oxen. Jenny couldn't hear the words Charlie uttered then, now she sensed his hurt and disappointment in her.

"Lord, help me," he pleaded. "Why must she take everything I say and make it sound wrong? Why can't she understand why we had to move? Help us get this blamed wagon going again, Lord." He knew she was not born to hard labor, but thought she would adjust as she realized the dream he hoped to share with her.

Pushing her head back with her effort to budge the wagon, Jenny knocked her bonnet off. As it fell into the mud she thought, "What's the use. How can I go on caring? We'll never get this thing going again, and I'll never have an occasion to wear a pretty bonnet anyway. In this God-forsaken country, what does it matter? That farm of Charlie's will be just another quagmire. I can't do it. I can't take any more of this."

The wagon moved with a sudden lurch, and she fell into the mud pushing the bonnet completely under. Charlie saw her ignominious fall, but once the wagon was going he led the team to the top of a rise before going back to rescue the screaming woman.

A loud piercing scream of despair escaped from Jenny's throat as she kicked and pounded her fists into the splashing mud. She was conscious of Charlie's gentle arms, more now as a ghost reliving the scene than when it actually happened. At the time of the experience her own misery over-rode all else. But now as her spirit absorbed all the feelings, she felt for Charlie, too, adding to her torment.

He lifted her and cradled her in his arms tenderly. Pushing her red curls, loose now that the bonnet was gone, back from her face, he tried to comfort her.

"Hush, my darling. It tears my heart out to see you like this. It won't always be this rough. Where we're going there will be big oak and pecan trees, almost like back home in Georgia. And little Temple won't get malaria there. Please, believe me and trust me. It's a beautiful, healthful country. Come on, Sweetheart. Hang on just a few more days."

She drew her fist back to hit him, but didn't have the energy. She wanted to go home. She wanted to sleep on a feather bed with clean white sheets! She wanted her beautiful clothes washed and ironed by her mother's slave, Bessie Lou. Why did that awful war have to come and change her life so completely?

Feeling the mud, and the older dirt and grime accumulated over a week when they didn't have enough water to bathe, Jenny shuddered and hated Charlie and this terrible country where it could be so dry one day and rain in floods the next.

From the back of the wagon came five-year-old Temple's cries as he was frightened awake by the commotion.

As the scene finally played itself out in her ghostly mind, Jenny wondered why she still could not forgive Charlie and love him just the way he was. She understood his motives for being determined to move to Texas. His two older brothers had been killed in the battle of Shiloh, and she knew he had suffered as his younger brother and the little sister who was so dear to him had died with the fever. She could see his mother now as she sat and rocked a little doll, unconscious of all around her. Her loss had been so great that she rejected reality for a more comfortable dream world, where nothing could ever hurt her again. Charlie chose a more practical escape. He wanted better for his family.

The ghost of Jenny clutched her baby to her breast and wandered in the gathering evening shadows. Two spirits locked together, appearing and disappearing, wandered up the creek bottom to the train track. Protecting her babe from supposed harm, feeling none of the thorns and switches that made no movement with their passing, Jenny wondered why it seemed important that she stop the train. An urgency not to be denied made her stand on the track as the train came around a grove of trees.

Alexander, in 1882, was a bustling shopping town for the surrounding community. It was connected to Fort Worth, about sixty miles east, by a much used railroad, had three banks and several stores. Homer Johnson and Walker Allen, the engineer and stoker of the train, the day Jenny tried her newly found power, were discussing the dangers of their jobs as they left the depot.

"You know, Homer, I suspect Alexander ain't as sleepy a little town as people suppose."

"What cha' got in mind, Walker? All kinds of people live around here."

"That's what I mean. I wouldn't be surprised if some of them train robbers that rob trains around Fort Worth and Dallas lived here mixed up with everybody else. They could take the train to the city, rob another train and be back here on the next round. Seems to me like this would be a good place to hole up." Homer was right proud of his theory. He checked his gauges again and pulled the warning whistle as they neared the crossing before Green's Creek.

"Just never know what to expect in this damn job. Old Jim Weems said they never suspected a thing last Monday until them robbers stuck guns in their faces." Walker said.

"Yeah. Times is scary. Seems like the whole country is jest a big festerin' boil. Look out!" He slammed on the brakes and blared the whistle automatically as he saw the woman on the tracks.

"That fool woman! I can't stop this here train that quick!" The brakes squealed and the two men in the engine cab held on to the hand holds. The four freight cars and the caboose buckled, rammed forward and then pulled back, teetering dangerously as the weight of the impact pulled to the outside of the curve. The man from the mail car had been passing the time of day with the brakeman in the caboose and was thrown against the door.

Homer and Walker in the cab watched in horror as the train ran over the woman with the baby in her arms. Sparks flew and wheels squealed against the rails as the train ate up the yards of track it took to stop. Almost before the noise finished echoing from car to car and from trees and rocks on the roadbed, Homer and Walker jumped the last step from the cab, one on one side and one on the other, and ran to the caboose, expecting at every step to find a head or decapitated body. They met the other two men behind the caboose.

"What in damnation! We couldn't have missed her," puzzled Homer.

"No, I swear I saw her go under the cow-catcher!" said Walker, his face several shades whiter than normal.

"What cha' talking about, Walker? Don't you know you might nigh killed me and Bob? Ain't even a crossing here!" said Jabe, the brakeman.

Bob was shaking his head, trying to regain his partially lost senses. "I could'a been the one you all are looking for. That door frame knocked the daylights out of me."

"They was a woman with a baby in her arms on the track! I had to stop!" said Homer.

Fear and anger mingled as the injured two faced the cabmen. Homer and Walker were still trying to understand what had become of the victims on the tracks. They stood there shaking their heads and wondering, but fear was the overriding power when a piercing scream battered their eardrums. Goose bumps prickled their necks and hair stood on ends as the scream filled the air. Then the shriek turned into peals of insane laughter! They turned and ran back to their places on the train and headed for Dublin with all possible speed.

Never did they forget that first encounter with Jenny's ghost. At first the four men were reluctant to tell of their experience, supposing they would be laughed at. But as others began to tell of seeing the ghost of Jenny, the train men enjoyed being the center of attention. After all, they figured that she chose them to be among the first ones to see her. Though the ghost often appeared on the tracks after that first night of terror, and they always attempted to stop, the first time was the grandaddy of all frights.

"Hereafter, perhaps, some intellect may be found
which will reduce my phantasm to the com-
monplace—some intellect more calm, more logi-
cal, and far less excitable than my own, which
will perceive, in the circumstances I detail with
awe, nothing more than an ordinary succession
of very natural causes and effects."
—EDGAR ALLEN POE
The Black Cat

CHAPTER II

The Way It Was

Jenny remembered Charlie as he had been when she first met him, just home from the Civil War. The horror he had witnessed and been a part of had etched his gaunt face with a haunting pain. The long chin seemed to get longer and the deep-set grey eyes more tormented as he viewed the destruction of the old home place which had been a battle ground. He was the only one of three brothers who did return—sometimes he wished he had not. Jenny sensed his anguish and tried to comfort him, to help him find some cause to smile, but rarely did he allow any happiness to rest in his soul. His long bony frame gave evidence of short rations. Short supplies from plantations laid waste by war presented no new problems to him, but the desolation ended his dreams. How could he ever rebuild? How could he ever live contentedly on land desecrated by the blood of his comrades? Then the sickness began. Jenny was glad when he found interest in wanting to start over somewhere other than Georgia, so she encouraged him to make the trip to Texas. She loved him beyond her love for home and a way of life she'd never know again.

The ghost of Jenny surveyed the acres she and Charlie had wrested from nature. Measuring each tree stump in her mind, counting again the hours of toil they'd spent making the land their own, Jenny floated from field to pasture, to creek and wood. Their hours of grubbing and cutting hadn't changed the general view much, except for the cabin and the twenty acres Charlie had cleared and plowed for corn and cotton. Now the weeds had reclaimed that. Pasture grasses followed the once plowed contours, now wild with yellow daisies nodding in the breeze. Purple thistles stood royally above other weeds, bending as if to instruct and direct lower orders of colors. Keith's cows grazed the pasture and set parameters for the brush under the oaks. Jenny's spirit measured her habitation with fierce possessiveness. Who would care now? Was it all for naught?

Charlie had made a trip to Erath County, Texas, two years before their move. Following the advice of a cousin of his father's, he had searched until he found just the place he wanted. Although the soft rolling hills, partially wooded but open enough to allow a view of the creek, were very different from Georgia, he felt a need to husband the unkept acres, unspoiled by war. A partially wooded track with a few big trees along the ridge about one hundred yards from the east bank of Green's Creek looked like paradise to him. He figured a cabin would "nestle real comfortable" under that huge live oak making a home to hold to. The old tree, full of years, would afford shade and a sense of permanence to their chosen spot.

Jenny remembered how proud Charlie was when they got in sight of the place in their covered wagon, he walking in front of Maud and Missy, as usual, with Old Rip, the yellow hound, following. She and Temple were riding on the seat, too heavy with weariness to notice the landscape. She absently swatted at the flies which rode with them, and Temple was counting the cottontail rabbits which Old Rip was too tired to chase. Jenny relived the scene as she watched herself and her family approach along the faint road worn by the few other settlers who were scattered in the vicinity and who went regularly, though seldom, to Alexander for supplies. Too tired to brace against the jolts of the ungiving wheels over the rough, rocky road, she jostled and swayed.

"There it is, Jenny! We're home! See that big live oak," Charlie was ecstatic. "And the slope beyond goes down to the creek. There's a hole of water just below the big tree yonder that never goes dry."

Jenny raised her bonnet with the back of her hand and looked with weary eyes. "Home? But there's nothing here, Charlie."

It wasn't that she was surprised to see the parcel of land with no improvements. Why was she so disappointed? She had known it would be that way. Charlie had told her. He had told her over and over about the untouched land he planned to claim, but it was hard to match reality with his dream. He had talked of nothing else since their marriage, describing the lay of the land, the hill where cool summer breezes blew, and the abundance of wildlife. They were going to Texas and they would carve their own farm out of the wilderness. He held up the hands that could do it. He would clean a small patch to farm that first year, trimming the trees he cut for logs for a cabin.

"Ain't it wonderful, Jenny! The cabin will be here with a barn for the animals right over there, and the first field to plant, come spring, right where those trees are. By planting time, I'll have that patch cleared and ready. Course, it won't be much the first year, but you just wait! We'll have the best little farm in Erath County before two winters are gone."

"Can't you see the love and pride in him? Can't you respond with just a little heart?" the ghost pleaded, seeing and feeling Charlie's happiness and the weary apathy of Jenny. That was her curse as a disembodied spirit: to be able to see and feel behind words and actions of the people who had been involved in her life. No chance to undo the deeds, but she must see again and again her mistakes and feel, too late, the pain they caused.

It was beautiful to Charlie! Like food to a starving man! He feasted his eyes. They had arrived in late October and the woods were a riot of color. The red oak and pin oak were absolutely scarlet on the sunny sides, not fading, but ripening to deeper maroon on the shady sides. Live oak and a few cedar broke the glow with their deep greens. The carpet of grass had turned to light toast color, but was still full of nutrition for the oxen. As the heavy wagon lumbered toward the big oak, Jenny's attention sparked a smidgen at the colors. She noticed, even in her weariness, a hem of brilliant sumac bordering the hill like a bright red ruffle around a circular skirt. Light yellow-green leaves of the willows still clung to trees along the creek. Climbing from branch to branch, mustang grapes made bowers of dark green in some places. The huge pecan tree, up from the bank far enough to offer a grand view to travelers who came to the creek for water and a few minutes rest, still held its leaves, though the carpet on the ground showed many had fallen along with an abundance of nuts.

Charlie's enthusiasm was contagious, and Jenny did get a little into his mood of things, though resentment continued to build inside. How could they ever survive a winter in that horrible covered wagon? As the weeks passed, she decided that surviving one day at a time was the only possible way to endure, so she kept busy. She picked up pecans, knowing they would taste good in the winter, especially in bread pudding. She found a few overripe grapes to make juice. Getting their camp organized with places for wood and water, rocks arranged best for cooking over a camp fire took some experimenting. Charlie built a wind shelter and thatched roof over the wagon, extending it several feet in front to help turn the rain and keep it from putting out their fire, but he could take very little time away from the land clearing process. He worked at it from daylight until dark, and Jenny worked just as hard, but without the heart. Her heart was longing for home back in Georgia where she envied her sister in the big plantation house with servants and clean linen and a fireplace to warm her bedroom.

They did endure. Jenny used a little gingham from her trunk to make a curtain for the only window the one-room cabin would have, and she helped Charlie fashion some three-legged stools from the trimmings he cut. He also made shingles, a very time consuming task with only a handsaw and an ax. They worked until dark and then slept in the cold icy wagon on top of wool batting and under two quilts and two hand woven wool coverlets, gifts from Jenny's family when they left Georgia. As she burrowed into the bed between Charlie and Temple, she hugged her slow burning anger at fate and resentment of hardship to her for warmth.

For a few days that winter the north wind was so cold and furious that they could do nothing but huddle in the wagon, except for trips out to build a fire and thaw water for themselves and the animals. Jenny thought winter would never end, but gradually, the cold spells got shorter and the sunshine warmer.

Almost every day Charlie managed to add a few logs to the pile for their cabin.

Neighbors, though none lived near, only one less than two miles away, knew when Charlie had enough logs ready for the cabin. With the coming of spring they came from miles around for a house raising. The men brought their tools, and knowing that Charlie probably didn't have enough, each brought a few shingles he had made for just such a purpose. The women brought food. None of it was fancy, since the winter had depleted everyone's pantries, but the fixings were wonderful. Jenny even made some fried pies from peaches they had brought from Georgia. Children, ready for warm weather and adventure, came to play with Temple while the work was going on.

"I aim to repay you fellers for your help some day. You see I ain't got much now, but someday—" Charlie promised, watching with amazement how the men knew just what to do and how to do it.

"That's all right, Charlie, I reckon we're having more than enough fun for pay. Does a heart good to come get to know good neighbors," said Franklin Gilstrap, shifting his hatchet to his other hand as he fitted a notched end of one log to another. His felt hat shaded his sharp grey eyes as he looked up to judge the level of the log.

"We had to get started, too. Besides, these ladies can really cook when they have occasion. Most times we get beans and cornbread and buttermilk. My woman forgets how to cook good stuff when it's jest us," Sam Keith added. He rubbed his ample belly under his bibbed overalls.

"You sure are one lucky feller, Charlie, having a wife who's good to look at and a dern good cook, too. Now take my Millie. I reckon they ain't no better cook in the country, but my Millie never were no belle of the ball to none 'cept me," said Franklin, his words contrary to the pride in his voice.

Sam laughed, "Bet she's the only one who'd put up with you, Franklin, don't you agree, Brownlow?"

Chester Brownlow was not the best worker of the group. He had little shifty brown eyes that never quite seemed to focus on anything, darting from one thing to another. His soft face sported a brown beard, neatly trimmed, hiding a small indifferent chin. His ample body was constantly moving in some manner, indicative of his high strung, nervous personality. Most of the time he watched the work and offered unappreciated advice, or sneaked off to sample what the women were cooking. Often his target was his wagon where he took frequent and long pulls from a jug hidden under a tow sack. He seemed to enjoy watching the cooks as they caught up on the woman talk that had gone unsaid all winter, and swapped stories about all those new-fangled products at the stores in Alexander.

Maybe it was because she remembered her own months of living in a covered wagon that Sally Keith knew what to do. With her flour sack apron covering a blue print dress, she directed the dinner preparations. She was tall, plain, blonde and full of talk, but always sensitive to the pain of others. While Chester was out advising the men and getting in the way, she spoke softly to his wife, Katherine.

"Did he do that to you?" asked Sally, touching the big ugly bruise that covered nearly all the left side of Katherine's face and disappeared into the edge of her hair.

"No, the old cow I was trying to milk knocked me against the barn," answered Katherine, covering the bruise with her hand and glancing to see where Chester was. She was small, a frail delicate woman wearing a carefully patched dress.

Sally didn't believe her. "How do you stand it? Why do you put up with it?" She was not one to let anyone run over her. Sam Keith just better not think of hitting his wife.

Katherine saw there was no use lying to Sally. "What else can I do?" she asked, ducking her head. She smoothed the faded apron over her stomach, swollen with child.

Sally noticed the paleness of her skin away from the angry bruise, "Are you sure it's OK?" Maybe it was her sadness that made Katherine look unhealthy. The skin was tight and drawn over the cheek bones. Blue blood vessels spread like webs from the angry bruise.

Katherine pointed to her five-year-old son. "I just hope this one's another boy. Most times he ain't so bad with the boy." Katherine talked with her head ducked and Sally could barely hear the words. She sighed as she patted the unhappy woman's arm, remembering the tenderness and protectiveness Sam showed when her own children were expected, and as they grew.

"Guess we better set the plates on the wagon," Sally said as she saw Chester look their way with suspicion.

One wagon, parked under the shade of a group of elms was the serving table. The ladies made coffee and poured it into tin cups. A pitcher of thick cream from last night's milk was next to the cups. They had water fresh from the creek or milk to drink, too. The pots of beans and turnip greens seasoned with salt pork, along with homemade hominy was stick-to-the-ribs goodness.

They were real neighbors. Remembering the hardships of the first year or two, each seemed to know everyone else's business, but they were not considered prying, just concerned. Each did his part to try to make the way easier for someone else.

Of course, there were some who were not so goodhearted. Crimes were committed, but the plague of the country was the vigilante groups. Feared by all and often swayed by power-seekers, they could spring up overnight.

It took only a day of combined effort to raise the one-room cabin. As the neighbors gathered their families and belongings into their wagons and headed for home, Charlie and Jenny surveyed their new home. After winter months of isolation, Jenny had been almost happy the day of the house raising. Being around people again awakened hope, and the thought of being able to move out of the wagon and under a roof was wonderful. The pull of the land and pride in ownership began to awaken in Jenny. She stood straight- backed and determined as she waved to Sally and Sam, the last to depart, since they had the shortest distance to go.

Life was hard. Having the dirt floor cabin didn't solve every problem, by any means, it just made some of the other problems show a little hope, and Jenny needed hope like a plant needs water. Being around the other women for the house raising made her realize how different she was. It seemed to her that Sally, Ruth Ann, Millie, and the others were happy with their rough life— except for Katherine. Maybe they never knew anything better. Surely they had never known the gracious life of a plantation, or they wouldn't be so content. They would be as homesick as she was. But she didn't know—or care—where all the settlers came from. She didn't even try to sort the good from the bad, as she could not imagine these people being really involved in her life. Her spirit, at the time, felt no kinship. But the ghost re-lived the wisdom and felt pride in the neighbors that day.

"Excuse me; I have no desire to be ridiculed as a
superstitious dreamer, nor, on the other hand,
could I ask you to accept on my affirmation
what you would hold to be incredible, without
the evidence of your own senses."

—EDWARD BULWER-LYTTON
The Haunters and the Haunted

CHAPTER III

Sally, A Friend

In such a short time, Charlie did not have much land ready for planting the first spring, in spite of pushing his lean body to the limit. He used the oxen hitched to the borrowed plow to make the furrows while Jenny and Temple dropped the seed corn. They planted beans and other vegetables on some of the land, knowing that they must grow most of their food. The hard work of picking wild plums and grapes, making jelly like Sally showed her, drying the beans and peas and heating them to kill the bugs, making and filling a root cellar with sweet potatoes, turnips, and potatoes kept Jenny busy. She felt a sense of pride in the store of food as she surveyed the fruits of her efforts.

A chimney was a rare thing in those early cabins, but the Papworth cabin had a stick and dirt chimney, the outside made of sticks with mud on the inside, a thick coat of sticky clay-mixed mud. Charlie finished it nights after the house raising. Jenny kept the dirt floor swept clean, taking care to sprinkle it down about every two days and gradually forming a hard surface.

"It's like fighting a never ending sandstorm," she muttered to herself, envious of Charlie's contentment.

Though she had thought she'd do anything, live anywhere if he could only find a little joy in life, she hadn't expected to live like this. Try as she might, it seemed impossible to take off shoes and get in bed without having grit between the sheets. She hated the dust and the grit in her bed.

"Wouldn't it be wonderful to have a floor," she said time and again to Charlie.

"Jenny, be reasonable. The lumber has to be hauled from a mill east of the Trinity River. We can't afford that. Besides, this ain't so bad."

Wooden floors were a part of the dream world. Charlie said that some day they would have a bigger house with floors and real glass windows. She had to admit that spending the winter in the cabin would be better than it was last winter in that cold wagon.

In spite of promises Charlie made and dreams he tried to share with her, Jenny could never grow accustomed to convenience being a wooden bucket of water hanging in the middle of the room from a joist in the rafters. A tin dipper stayed in the bucket and all thirsty comers drank from the same dipper. Jenny used the left-over water every morning to cook with, and washed the bucket and dipper every day, but they never seemed clean to her. She found, as she began to visit a little, that their cabin was very much like others in the community. One corner of the room was the kichen where the polished copper cooking utensils hung on the wall. Jenny had only four, but she noticed that each woman visitor seemed to automatically look to see that the copper displayed a proper sheen. On a shelf under the pans was a meager supply of groceries: the soda, salt, sugar, lard bucket, and underneath the shelf was the meal barrel. Some kind of box in which to store meat was also under the shelf. Usually the meat box held only pork jowl or belly in salt.

Atop the meat box was the usual place for a wooden tray holding knives and forks. Charlie carved some spoons from cedar that winter while he rested by the fire. Most spoons were hand carved wooden ones, and the handles for the knives were often made of corn cobs. That's the way the Papworth cabin was fitted, and it was the same with others, even some that had been built several years earlier. Seems the men concentrated first on outside improvements such as barns, bigger fields, livestock. Only in the winter did they sometimes turn their attention to things the women wanted.

A sure fixture in such cabins was the gunrack on the wall near the door. The Winchester was the family's chief source of meat, and occasionally was needed for protection. In the corner farthest from the door, was the bed. Charlie and Jenny were proud of the bedstead they had brought from Georgia. Though they had no springs under the shuck mattress, the frame was laced with rope, and her wool bat was a godsend. At least, a few of the spiders and centipedes were frustrated by it being off the floor. That winter Charlie made a cot for Temple that fitted at the end of their bed.

The walls of the cabin were logs fitted as close together as possible with mud and straw stuffed in the cracks. On the wall behind the bed, hanging from wooden pegs, were the extra clothes for the family. Few pegs were needed since one change of everyday and the Sunday best made up their entire wardrobe. Jenny's trunk, with many scars and scratches to show it had made the trip across rivers and prairies, held winter things during the summer, and one beautiful white blouse with rows and rows of handmade lace and little pearl buttons. Some days, when the world seemed too heavy to bear, Jenny took the blouse out and caressed it with her red, calloused hands, then sighed and hid it from sight again.

The tedium was broken late that first summer when three older men and a boy who spoke Spanish came looking for a lost mine, or buried Spanish bullion. They were very secretive about what they hunted on a place adjoining Charlie's farm. Jenny fairly bristled when they strayed across their boundary.

"Charlie Papworth, you better tell them coyotes to keep off our land. No stranger's gonna dig here," she said waving her broom in the doorway.

Chester Brownlow took the opportunity to come for a visit to the Papworth cabin. He convinced them the mine was nearer the creek.

"Them bastards wanted to dig on my land, but me and Betsy here," he patted his shotgun, "persuaded them that really wasn't what they wanted." Chester grinned, showing a missing front tooth among others stained yellow with tobacco. His little eyes seemed to touch every part of her person as he looked at Jenny. She shivered and went back into the house leaving Charlie and Chester talking by the water barrel. She remembered Katherine's bruised face and spirit.

Charlie bought a horse when he took his corn to trade day in Dublin. Jenny could ride. As a child she had slipped off to the stable and got Old Ned to let her ride her mother's horse. In Texas, she felt a little more freedom when she could ride to a neighbor's occasionally, and she shocked all the people who saw her because she rode with her husband's saddle rather than a sidesaddle. But they could not afford two, and she certainly was not going to let a few wagging tongues take the pleasure of riding from her. She became an excellent rider, and often rode over to Mrs. Keith's to learn how to do all the many tasks she never dreamed had to be done. Learning how to preserve food for the winter, which wild plums were good for; jelly and how to make it, finding a pattern for Temple's shirt, which was her second, after the curtain, sewing project, were complicated puzzles to her.

Putting the memory of a carriage with a liveried driver to follow her directions behind her, Jenny made a real adventure of her first visit to the Keiths'. With Temple on the horse behind her, Jenny crossed the creek at the shallow above the deep hole of water, and followed the wagon tracks to the Keith house on the next farm. It was only two miles, but hundreds and eons from her dreams of reality.

Up the hill and through the pasture she even noticed the wildflowers along the border of wood as she startled a covey of quail. The morning sun on her bonnet gave her a cozy feeling. She breathed deeply of the clean air wondering if microbes could hide in it as they did back in Georgia. As she tied the horse's reins to a limb of the oak tree in front of the cabin, a familiar fragrance tingled her nose and teased her memory. Looking toward the cabin, she felt her heart flutter as she found the source. Sally had nurtured a lilac bush by the door. Doubtless her used water went to the tree and to the morning glory vine climbing strings Sally had stretched up to the window and over to the door.

When the older woman came to the door, Jenny wondered again at her age. She had probably been the same plain woman all her life, but her blue eyes twinkled with warmth and friendliness. Her mousy blonde hair, slicked back in a bun on the back of her head, made her short pug nose and long chin more prominent than necessary. Sally was a big woman with a hearty, ready laugh that endeared her to young children. She was wearing an old navy blue printed dress with a bib apron tied over it.

"Why, hello, Jenny. Do come in. And Temple, just look how long your legs are. You'll soon be riding by yourself. I'm so glad you came to see me." Sally shook out her apron as if she had come to the door for that purpose. She had been snapping beans when she heard the horse come up. She patted Temple on the head and invited them in.

"Thank you Mrs. Keith. I thought you might would help me with this shirt I'm trying to make for Temple. I'm afraid I don't know much about sewing." Jenny noticed how Sally's eyes were the color of the morning glories, true blue and honest. Then Jenny realized that Sally might be a rather attractive woman under other circumstances.

"Do call me Sally, and I'll call you Jenny. Truth is, you remind me of my own daughter, Marie. She lives in Fort Worth, now. Married a railroad man. Sure, I can help you with a shirt. Made many a one."

Jenny's eyes were immediately attracted by brass pots and pans hanging on the far wall. A plank table with a long bench on the back side and two cane bottomed chairs, one at the end and one on the side near the end, sagged from years of use. Tears touched her lashes as Jenny noticed the wildflowers in the crock cream pitcher on the table. That was a touch of home. She hadn't seen a flower in a vase since the day she left Georgia. She remembered Bessie Lou bringing a vase of daisies to the table that day. That tidbit of memory made Jenny feel at ease on this, the first of many visits.

But none of the women knew what to do about the Granddaddy Longleg spiders that soon made their homes in the rafters and rough shingles of the roofs of the cabins. The Papworth cabin had no ceiling and before the first summer was over the spiders and centipedes had come in out of the wild to make their homes with the humans. The huge centipedes, much larger than those found in later years, were the natural enemy of the granddads. Often a real stampede of granddads was stirred up when a few centipedes got hungry, and clumps of them would fall into the bed, on the floor, into the frying pan, whatever happened to be underneath the war of the rafters.

Jenny shivered as she told Mrs. Keith about her loathing of the insects. "Yesterday, a bunch of the horrible creatures fell right in the pan! The whole house stunk instantly as they roasted! The pan was hot, but fortunately I hadn't put the grease in. What can I do, Mrs. Keith?" She threw up her hands in a gesture of helpless despair.

"Not much you can do, Honey. I've tried everything! I tried lighting some shucks and burning them out one time, but I almost caught the house afire. I'll never try that again."

"But how do you stand it? Sometimes they crawl over my face when I'm asleep! I just want to scream!" said Jenny shuddering.

"I know. I might nigh scared Sam to death one night right after we moved. Something skittered over my face in the dark and I screamed bloody murder! I guess I've gotten used to the feel by now. I just sorta brush them off without waking," said Mrs. Keith.

"I'll never get used to it!" said Jenny, shivering again as she imagined the feel of the scampering insects on her skin. Then she remembered, "I keep dipping them out of the water. What if I took a drink without looking! I heard Charlie spitting the other night when he got up in the dark to get a drink. I asked him what was the matter and he just grunted, but I know he got a spider in his mouth. How do you stand it?"

"Well, now, I guess they're harmless. Never heard of one hurting nobody. Might hurt themselves trying to get out of the way. Now them centipedes are something else. They can really hurt a body." Sally rubbed her leg as she remembered a sting. "Always be sure to shake out your clothes before you put them on in the mornings. Sam had one of them critters in his pants one morning when he forgot to shake them before he put them on. That centipede stung him a good one. I couldn't help but laugh at him hopping around on one leg trying to get out of them pants. 'Course, he got mad at me for laughing, but you should've seen him hopping around here. Tain't easy to hop with a belly as big as Sam's."

Jenny managed to smile as she pictured Sam Keith hopping around hollering and stumbling. But she knew she would never get used to spiders in her dinner plates and centipedes an ever present threat. She thought of the beautiful table in Georgia, set with the chinaware and crystal and white linen. If only that stupid war hadn't ruined everything.

The ghost of Jenny looked in on all the early scenes and bemoaned the lost chances for happiness. If only she had been more patient. Other women learned to stand the hardships and keep their sanity. The love and pride of the homely Sally Keith aroused a hunger in the restless spirit. Floating about all the familiar places, she longed to touch, to caress Temple as she had never done in life. She thought of his blonde hair with the cowlick that made a twig at the crown stand straight up, especially when he had gone to bed with it damp. The memory of his big smile with missing front teeth and the little giggle as he played with the dog awakened the love she had suppressed in life. For once, the longing and torment were greater than the anger.

"Then all of a sudden she was seized by a vague
dread of the unknown. She had closed the door
behind her on entering and as she stood alone
in the long silent room, her dread seemed to
take shape and sound, to be there breathing and
lurking among the shadows."

—EDITH WHARTON
Afterward

CHAPTER IV

Home Alone

The ghost prowled restlessly, hungrily examining with burning eyes the wild plum thicket between the creek and railroad. Then she floated over the creek and through the pasture, irresistibly drawn to the cabin. She was haunted by the discontent she had experienced with her family there, and wondered at its burden. Charlie had not brought her to Texas against her will. She had wanted to come. Nothing was right in Georgia. The discontent had not been Texas born. The plantation had been sold for taxes and her parents lived on in a few rooms of the big house only because no one else wanted it. Upkeep was impossible without servants, and without slaves cotton was impractical. But her heart had refused to follow reason. She had pictured Texas as Georgia had been before the war, never as the uncivilized land it was. Gradually her dreams had begun to adjust before that letter came. She saw again the trouble that piece of paper had brought.

Jenny begged Charlie not to go. They had been living on the farm about two years. The baby, Mary Jean, had been born in

December with Mrs. Keith there to help. Sally stayed with Jenny for a few days, and Charlie tried to help, though the best he did was stay out of the way. Although Jenny was scared, she quickly allowed motherhood to occupy her time and consciousness. She sang and talked to the baby as she managed all the washing and cooking and cleaning for her household. She fought even harder to rid the cabin of bugs and spiders, and slept with the baby hugged close to protect her from centipedes and the little lizards that came in for the bugs. There seemed no way to keep other life- forms away. The one window, which had to be open for the air in the spring and summer gave ready access to all the uninvited guests. No problem for lizards to run up the log wall and through the window. They even came down the chimney when the fire burned low. Though Jenny swept under the bed and all around carefully each day, she was sure some kinds of horrible creatures had hidden dens. The fact that Charlie and Temple paid no attention to the things that made Jenny shiver with revulsion, made no sense to her. How could they ignore the dirty pests? Protecting her baby from chance encounters be-came almost an obsession. She longed for her family to see the baby. "I wish your grandmother Washburn could see you. She would love you. Such a perfect little beauty," she crooned to the child. "But she would really have a fit if she saw how we live in this backwards country. Creepy crawly things just waiting to pounce on you." Thinking of how Charlie laughed at her fear of bugs and little crawling things, she frowned.

Using a stick to punch the flour sack diapers boiling in lye soapy water in a pot hanging over the fire, she said to herself, "Bet mama never washed diapers for us." It was a daily task because she had so few. "Always had Negroes around to do that. And cooking over a fireplace? She might soil her fingers." She had mixed feelings about mama who delegated responsibility, but she remembered being cuddled by Aunt Bessie Lou who was always there to comfort her with her softly spoken words and a tender smile on her chocolate brown face. Shaking off the memories Jenny said, "Temple, I need another bucket of water."

Charlie hauled the water from the creek in two wooden barrels in the wagon. Sometimes she thought he begrudged the time it took to keep her supplied, so she tried to be saving with it. They went to the creek to bathe when the days were hot and still. Charlie and Temple nearly always bathed and swam in the creek, but so did fish and snakes and no telling what all. Jenny could seldom be persuaded to go with them. However, she was learning to stretch the water. After the baby's bath she rinsed the previous day's supply of diapers in that water, then she emptied the pan on the only flower, a florabunda rose Mrs. Keith had given her with instructions about how to make the most of carried water. Her own bath water was used to sprinkle the floor and settle the dust.

Temple was big enough to dip water out of the barrel for her, which was a good thing since it saved her from seeing the insects and other creatures that might have drowned trying to drink. They had wooden covers for the barrels to keep trash from blowing in, but invariably, a few little insect legs would be turned up. Charlie had arranged a stump by the water barrels for Temple to stand on to reach the water as the level went down. He also had two other stumps arranged, one to hold a bucket of water with a tin dipper, and the other for a washpan so that he could wash his face and hands before entering the cabin—when the water wasn't frozen over. He did try to make life a little easier for Jenny, though he lost patience with never being able to satisfy her wants.

Seven-year-old Temple was proud of his little sister, but he did think she took a lot of attention. He had to stay around the cabin to help his mother sometimes when he would rather be out in the field with his dad or down on the creek fishing.

In the spring, a message came for Charlie from his family in Georgia. Both his parents were dead and he had inherited a share of the farm equipment and household goods. But he would have to make a trip back there to get the load. His uncle had loaded Charlie's share in a wagon, and there was a team of horses to pull the wagon, but no one was available to drive it to Texas.

"Jenny, I guess I'll go home next week to get the supplies," he said, making plans in his mind about how to do it, and when he could best be spared from his farming.

"You mean 'we' don't you, Charlie?" said Jenny.

"No, babe. We have enough money for one train ticket. Guess I'll have to be the one that goes to help settle the estate and drive the wagon back."

"But you can't leave me here by myself," Jenny was outraged. She hadn't even considered being left alone on the farm.

"Well, now. You'll have Temple to help you with the chores and he can keep his eyes on little Mary Jean for you sometimes." Charlie said.

"But I want to go home and see my mama. She ain't dead."

"I wish we could all go, Jenny. But someone has to stay here. We don't even have the title to this place yet. It wouldn't be safe to leave it with no one here, even for a month, and I have to go sign papers and drive the wagon back."

"Charlie, I'm scared. No telling what might happen in this God-forsaken country. Sally Keith was telling me about some Indians that came through last week."

"They were just passing through, Babe. I spoke to them when they came by the McDow hole to water their horses. It was when I was down there getting water last week. They were real friendly." Charlie didn't tell her he had seen them several times. They usually avoided the cabins. He thought they were harmless. Heck, they were watering at that hole hundreds of years before the settlers came.

Jenny's eyes were glittering with anger. "What do you know, Charlie Papworth! You think you know everything! You don't know all the Indians in the world. Besides, you've got no idea of how lonesome it can be around here."

Charlie had learned from experience that he may as well let her go on for awhile. He just dropped his hands and listened helplessly.

"What do you know about all the people around here, anyway! Some of the ones that visit here give me the creeps."

"Now, now, honey. You know we've got good neighbors. Why, they have gone out of their way to be good to us. Sally Keith is probably the best friend you could ever have. Better than those stuck up folks in Georgia that thought you were crazy to marry me and come to Texas."

"Sally's all right. But she's about the only one. And don't you talk about my friends back home. At least, they were smart enough to stay away from here!"

"It's just because you know Sally best, and she lives close enough to call on when you need her. The others are just as good if you'd just try to make friends," said Charlie.

"That's what you think! That Brownlow man is evil. Sally says he beats his wife and kid. And what about Stevens? That crackpot gets drunk and insults everybody around. I can't stay here alone."

"Look, Jenny, I have to go. Just think of what a help a good plow will be, and a team of horses. What a difference that will make! Jenny, there are things there dad left me it would take years for me to save money and buy. And furniture! Why you will even have a chiffonier!"

"What good will that be! We don't even have a place to put it. And whoever heard of a chiffonier on a dirt floor," Jenny said, throwing her hands up, palms out, slinging her hair back and stomping her foot in a ritual of anger.

Seeing he could not persuade her to see things his way Charlie said, "Look, Jenny. You really have no choice. I'm going next week. Now that the crops are in I have to go and get back in time to plow and tend them. It'll take about four weeks to drive that team back. You will be fine here in the daytime and the Keiths said you could ride over and sleep at their place."

"Charlie Papworth! You mean to tell me you discussed our business with them before you did with me!" Jenny was outraged. He had been making plans even before talking with her. It was more than she could stand.

"All right! Go!" she stamped her foot and pounded him on the chest with her clenched fists as he tried to comfort her. "I wish I had never seen this place! If I went to Georgia now, I'd never come back. I hate you for going and leaving me. I hate you! I hate you! Just go on and make your old plans. I'll do as I please, and if anything happens to me you'll be sorry!"

Charlie did leave the next week. The quarrel between him and Jenny didn't get any better before he had to go, and he didn't like leaving her angry at him. What could he do? She was silent and sullen as he made his preparations and gave her instructions about everything. He took the early morning train. Temple rode on the horse behind him to Alexander so he could ride the horse back.

Alternately, Jenny fumed and pouted—and hated herself for doing so. Why couldn't she take things in stride? Why must she get so angry and upset? It never did any good. She butted her head against the inevitable with as much effect as a goat butting a rock mountain. She hated to go to the Keiths' at night because her ill temper made both them and her uncomfortable, but she was too frightened to stay in the cabin. For a week the arrangement worked, though awkwardly. She milked the cow, tended the other animals, did the usual chores, and then rode the horse with the baby in her arms and Temple behind her to the Keiths' for the night.

As they rode back to the cabin the last morning Jenny suspected from his breath odor that Temple had a sore throat. He had bad tonsils and several times a year would be sick with tonsillitis. The dread of her child's illness occupied her mind, reminding her of her helplessness. As soon as they got to the cabin she would make a gargle. Temple took the horse to the lot while she put Mary Jean in the crib Sally had loaned her when the baby was born.

As soon as Temple came to the cabin, Jenny stopped him at the door, "Turn and face the light, Temple. Let me look at your throat." Just as she suspected, his tonsils were swollen and red. She felt his forehead.

"My! They look awful! Like as not, you'll be running fever in an hour. Come to the door and gargle with this. Make sure you let it get way down on those tonsils, now."

Temple gargled, gagged, sputtered and shuddered. "Ugh, Mama, do you know how awful that is?"

"Yes, son. I know it's bad. But maybe it will make your throat better. Did you use all of it?'

As he nodded she said, "Now, just lay down and be quiet for a bit."

It didn't get better. As the day wore on, Temple's fever escalated, and by evening he was very sick. Jenny bathed his face and tried to keep him covered. He thrashed about on the bed sick and miserable until about dark when he finally slept. Jenny was scared. Not just about Temple's illness, but because he couldn't possibly make the trip to the Keiths' that night.

"Why, he couldn't even hold on. How could I ever get him there even if I didn't have Baby Jean, too. I'll have to stay here." She muttered to herself with a sense of dread.

Standing in the doorway, watching a haze settle like a shroud over the clearing, Jenny tried to decide if darkness crept up from the horizon or blended down from above. The colors of the dying sun were hidden behind thick clouds, giving no hint of the earlier fairness of the day. She didn't know whether to light the lamp and advertise her being there, or to stay in the dark. A nameless dread enveloped her, descending like a miasma settling at its source as she sat in the dark cabin. Jenny almost screamed as an owl hooted in the tree. Quickly she shut the door, but felt no security as she reached for the baby crib and listened to Temple's heavy breathing.

After a while, she roused herself and lit the lamp. "Can't be any worse than sitting here in the dark expecting a lizard to crawl up my leg."

It must have been nearly twelve o'clock when the knock on the door came. Jenny was not surprised. It was as if she were expecting the inevitable. Fear, because the intensity of the emotion could not be retained for so long, had produced a trance-like state. She went to the door cradling a faint hope that Sam Keith was worried about her and had come to see why she had not arrived at their house. But the hope died before it lived.

The man at the door said, "Hello, Jenny. I thought you might be getting lonesome," the whiskey on his breath made her flinch as he tried to see behind her. The dim lamplight revealed nothing beyond the lamp itself. In front was the chair Jenny had been sitting in, still rocking, and the baby crib.

"You can't come in!" said Jenny, trying to shut the door. The insolence in his voice was heavy and insulting, but the foot in the door was unmoving. He did come in.

"Now, now, Jenny. You know you're lonesome, and I'm not such a bad guy." He reached for her and as she dodged she knocked the crib over, spilling Mary Jean onto the floor. As the baby let out a startled scream, Jenny's trance was broken. She kicked and shoved the man back to the door and rescued the baby. The enraged man came back fighting. Even in his state of drunkenness he knew that the woman was now and forevermore a danger to him.

Trying to throw her on it he hit the bed with a jolt that knocked Temple over behind it where he lay in fright and half unconscious with fever. The uneven fight between the strong enraged man and the small mother fighting for the life of herself and her children was short and brutal. Deathly silence prevailed as the man half crawled to his horse, mounted after a struggle, and rode down the lane.

"When the murder was first discovered, no suspicion fell—or, I ought rather to say, for I cannot
be too precise in my facts, it was nowhere
publicly hinted that any suspicion fell—on the
man who was afterwards brought to trial."
—CHARLES ALLSTON COLLINS and CHARLES DICKENS
The Trial for Murder

CHAPTER V

Vigilantes

E rath County was noted for its vigilantes. The reputation
probably started with a man named John R. Baylor, who,
by about 1859, had organized over four hundred men to wreak
vengeance on the Indians. Their purpose, according to Baylor,
was to exterminate the reservation Indians in Texas.

In the 50's several reservations were organized, and there
was promise of life in peace between settlers and Indians. The
Comanches raided both settlers and reservations, but in many
cases outlaw groups of Anglos disguised as Indians caused
unnecessary friction between the two groups who wanted only
to farm in peace.

In 1859, hundreds of people gathered in Stephenville to join
Baylor's vigilante army. A reward was offered for the scalp of a
man named Neighbors, an Indian Agent who had lived with the
reservation Indians trying to help them adjust, to improve their
ability to grow their own food and survive in confinement.

In defiance of the U. S. Army, Baylor led an attack on a
reservation, killing an elderly Caddo woman working in her

garden and an old man tending horses. The U. S. troops arrived and drove Baylor off, but the rescue was temporary. Baylor vowed to return with more recruits in six days.

Because of Baylor, the Indians were uprooted from their homes again and moved to Oklahoma. The original purpose of vigilantes in Erath County disappeared, but the sense of power led unscrupulous men to adopt other excuses for wearing hoods to protect their identity and take the law into their own hands. Various groups formed to catch horse thieves and other outlaws, and to commit many crimes themselves in the name of justice. It was fear tactics. No one dared protest because their neighbor on the next farm might be a member. One brave county sheriff who took office in the 70's, determined to gain legal control of crime in the county, was soon shot in the back by vigilantes in Stephenville.

Since the county seat of Erath County was Stephenville, the county sheriff was there. To cover the entire area adequately was impossible. He could not visit all the settlements in his county in a week by traveling on horseback. Circuit rider preachers had the advantage over the sheriff. They might be late for a funeral, but their subject wasn't going anywhere. The sheriff's subjects were changing locations as rapidly as possible. So the vigilantes thrived, and men with private grudges joined groups, accused an enemy of a crime, and wrought vengeance.

Charlie came riding home from Georgia late one evening in the summer. Sam Keith had cleaned the cabin as best he could, setting things in order after the murder and was there to meet Charlie and break the sad news to him. He heard the wagon coming over the rough road and watched sadly as joy and hope faded quickly from the tired face.

Expecting to see Jenny and the children waiting for him,

Charlie knew something was wrong when he came into view of his farm and there stood Sam Keith with a sober look on his face. The picture he had held in his mind for days of Jenny with the babe in her arms and little Temple by her side waving to him, had kept him moving when weariness demanded he stop.

"What's wrong Sam? Where's Jenny?" he asked as he jumped to the ground.

"I have bad news, Charlie. Temple's over at the house with Sally. Jenny and the babe were murdered about two weeks ago."

"Murdered! But why, Sam?" He ran into the house, unable to believe that they were not there.

Sam told him all they knew about the murder. With Charlie in a daze, Sam took care of the horses and other chores as he had been doing for two weeks. Then he took Charlie in his buggy to Alexander and showed him the fresh grave in the little church yard.

"We buried them together, Charlie, thinking that's the way you and Jenny would've wanted it. We couldn't keep them any longer. Sally dressed her in that pretty white blouse that was in the trunk." It was a long painful speech for Sam. He thought all his own tears had been shed earlier, but Charlie's pain brought more.

Giving Charlie a little time alone by the grave, Sam waited in the buggy. Then, he went to his friend and led him to the buggy. Not much was said on the way to the Keiths.

"And Temple?" Charlie was afraid to ask.

"He's all right. He had a real bad sore throat when we found him."

"Thank God. How did he escape?"

"We don't rightly know, Charlie. Sally thinks the sore throat was what kept them home that night. We found him under the bed. Maybe the murderer didn't see him."

Every day and night for the next couple of weeks Sam, Sally and Charlie tried to solve the mystery of who murdered Jenny. "Maybe it was a vigilante group," said Charlie.

"No. I don't think so. A man would come alone to do that kind of dirty work. And we didn't find a bunch of horse tracks. 'Course it was dry, but even so a dozen or so horses would have left signs." said Sam.

"We don't think it was Indians, either," said Sally. "The ones that visit you and Sam would never do something like that. Indians pass the word about who their friends are. Why, there hasn't been a Comanche raid in Dublin and down this way since the preacher helped that hungry Indian in 1870."

"Sally's right. Guess that was before you came, Charlie. It's been about ten years ago." Sam kept talking, in part to distract Charlie. "A Comanche Indian lost his bow when he was out on a hunt or scouting by hisself. He was getting right hungry, probably was on his way back west and hadn't eaten for several days. He was probably scared, too, because he was by hisself and so many settlers around. He rushed into a cabin on Armstrong Creek and grabbed food off a family's table. People just stood back and watched him eat they was so surprised. The man was a Baptist preacher named Ross. He took the Indian to Dublin and saw that he was treated kind. My brother Bill took him in for a couple of days until he was strong again, then the Indian went on his way. As he left he promised that there would be no more Comanche raids in Dublin, and there hasn't been to this day."

"No, I don't think it was an Indian either. But I sure wish to God I did know who the mean devil was. I've been asking around up at Jake's. He usually takes note of suspicious characters. But he ain't seen nothing unusual, nor heard anything."

"Guess I ain't got no advice fer you, Charlie. I jest don't know how you can stand to live in that cabin no more," said Sally.

"Well, we don't have much choice. Temple sure is scared to be around there. I appreciate you letting me and him sleep in your barn. It's going to take awhile before he wants to stay the night in the cabin, if he ever does. Maybe I should just sell my supplies and leave."

"I hate to see you do that. It's such a nice little place. You have a good corn patch and that cotton looks like it will make real good," said Sam.

"Yep, I plan to start gathering the corn tomorrow. Anyway, guess I'll try a little longer. 'Bout time for bed now. Come on, Temple, let's check the horses and hit the hay." Charlie stretched and yawned hoping he could sleep as he decided to turn in. "Need to get an early start tomorrow."

The next day Charlie and Temple were busy gathering corn. Temple sat on the wagon seat and held the horses' reins while Charlie yanked the full, dry ears from the stalks and threw them in the wagon. It didn't take much effort to control the horses. They were old hands at this game, having gathered corn in Georgia for several years.

By mid morning the sun was high and hot. The musty smell of the dust disturbed by the yanking mixed with the minute particles of shucks, silks, leaves, and sweat from man and animals twitched Temple's nose which was red from being rubbed. The chaff made him itch all over, and he was tired of sitting. When his dad stopped to wipe the sweat from his face and drink some water from the jug wrapped with wet burlap to help keep it cool, he was glad to jump down from the wagon.

"Pa, could I go to the creek and wade a little?" he asked.

"Well, now, son. That sounds like a good idea. Reckon you

know to stay in the shallows above the deep hole."

"Sure, Pa. Maybe I can find some crawfish under the rocks."

"That's a good idea. Take that extra bucket on the bench by the cabin and put some in it. We might set a trot line tonight and catch a catfish."

Temple stepped into the shallow water. It felt so good and cool. He rolled his pant legs up above his knees and wiggled his toes in the loose gravel on the bottom. He was too fast on the first flat rock he lifted. A cloud of dirt muddied the water so that he couldn't see a crawfish if there had been one. And it was a little deep to reach one hand down in front for the crawfish to see and try to evade, while the other hand grabbed it behind on the hard part of the back just behind where the claws attached. His daddy had shown him many times how to catch the dangerous looking critter so that he couldn't reach his hand to pinch. Temple waded to the edge where he could be more successful and soon had three crawfish, just the right size for a channel cat, swimming in the bucket. He was getting to be an expert. He had caught three crawfish in the last five attempts and raised up to yell to his pa.

Temple didn't yell. When he raised up he saw monsters riding horses coming up to his pa. Charlie, hearing the approaching horses— sounded like a whole army—was standing waiting to see what in tarnation they were doing. Temple hunkered down below the bank out of sight. Fear which had just begun to abate from his earlier experience made him tremble. He swallowed over the lump in his throat, wanting to run to his pa, or run toward the Keiths' or run somewhere, but he couldn't. He inched his head up to see through the grass and briars, but was invisible to the men. Not much talking was going on.

He heard his pa say, "Hell, no! I didn't steal them horses.

They belonged to my pa. I jest got back from Georgia with them."

"Look like stolen horses to me. You're one of the gang that's been stealing horses down near Hico, so shut up and get on that horse," said one of the men who seemed to be in charge. They were too busy to worry about anyone seeing them anyway.

There were thirteen men with hoods over their heads, eye-holes cut out to see, with guns. Most kept their guns trained on six other men with their hands tied behind their backs, but four were threatening his pa with shotguns.

Temple watched as one of the men unhitched the horses from the wagon. One man tied Charlie's hands behind his back after they made him get on a horse. With hooded men leading seven horses with riders who had their hands tied behind them, the gruesome party rode to the big pecan tree near the bank just a few yards from where Temple was hiding.

Temple watched in horror as seven of the men rode under a big limb and threw ropes with nooses over it. They pulled the ropes tight then others pushed guns into the backs of the tied men while the first seven took the horses' reins and led them under the limb. They worked together as if it were a well practiced routine. No words were spoken until the seven captives were sitting their horses with nooses around their necks.

Then the leader said, "You may as well confess fer the record. It don't really matter. We know you are all guilty as sin, but now is your chance. You have ten seconds."

Temple shuddered as the man spoke. The voice, though muffled by the hood, sounded familiar and made him even more afraid. What could he do?

The hooded man said, "Time's up!" as whips hit the rumps of the horses. Thirteen hooded men rode off without a backward glance.

Temple stared for a second at the seven men hanging from the limb. His pa was on the end of the limb, and his toes dragged the ground. He had to get him down!

Quick as a squirrel Temple was up the bank and running to the tree. That tree was an old friend that Temple had climbed many times. He reached for the holds with knowing fingers and bare toes, slipping once and almost falling. He reached the limb and began to crawl out on it holding to smaller branches from a limb above for balance. He reached his pa and tried to untie the rope. No way. It was big and stiff and tight. What to do?

He turned to go back down then grabbed a limber branch above and swung to the ground. Running to his pa he reached up to get his pocket knife out of his pants pocket. He could reach the pocket with his finger tips, but he was not tall enough to reach down into the pocket to the knife. Choking back the tears and the helpless cry that sprang to his lips he reached his pa's belt and managed to unbuckle it. Fortunately the top button of the pants was missing. Temple grabbed hold and started to yank, then something told him that would choke his pa more. Gently he unbuttoned another button and let the pants drop.

Where was that knife! He first looked in the wrong pocket, but then he found it. Other times he would not have been able to open it, but he didn't even stop to think he couldn't. He broke fingernails, but finally had it open and held it in his teeth as he climbed back up the tree and out to the end of the limb. He thought he could never saw through the rope. Fortunately, his added weight bent the limb a little more and Charlie's feet were firmer on the ground. At last he knew the rope was cut when his pa hit the ground. He scampered down the tree and cut Charlie's hands loose. Charlie had enough strength to remove the noose himself.

Charlie couldn't talk. Nor did he have strength to climb the tree. He signaled for Temple to go back up and cut the other ropes. One of the men breathed for a few minutes and then died. The others were dead before they hit the ground.

The vigilantes had taken the horses. As soon as Charlie bathed his face and gained a little strength they walked to Keiths'. Sam saw them coming along the cow trail to the creek.

"What in tarnation!" he asked as Charlie collapsed at his feet. "Sally! Sally! Come help me, girl." He yelled toward the house. Charlie struggled to his feet with Sam's help.

"Temple, child! You're white as a sheet! What happened?" As Sally gathered him in her arms she shuddered and began to cry.

"My daddy! My daddy can't talk!"

"It's all right. It's all right, now. You're safe now," Sally soothed.

Charlie managed to croak, "He saved my life. They hung me!"

With some hot coffee and some of Sally's ointment for the rope burn, Charlie soon was able to tell the story. They decided that staying there was too dangerous. Some of the vigilantes were bound to come looking for him as soon as they realized he didn't die. Charlie borrowed a horse from Sam and with Temple on behind him, set out for Oklahoma Territory before daybreak the next morning. They rode by the cabin for one last look, but didn't get off the horse.

"It seems like I can almost see your mother, Temple, standing there with little sister in her arms," said Charlie through the sadness that gripped him.

He watched as in the cabin doorway Jenny almost materialized — and then faded again. Charlie thought it was his imagination. Temple wasn't so sure as he clung to the reality of his pa's waist. He saw the water barrel where he had so often grumbled as he stretched to dip the water. He didn't answer his pa, but fear lumped in his throat.

"Seeing that cabin from the lane here sure makes me wish we could stay. I can almost feel her presence, like when she was in a gentle mood. See yonder," he pointed. "Looks like her in a white dress standing in the door."

But he didn't trust his eyes and his hand automatically went to the rope burn on his throat. Temple smothered a sob and shuddered as he thought of the horrors he had survived there. Crowded out were any happy memories he had about the home place.

Charlie, aware of the boy's discomfort, said, "I can't live with no ghost! Even if her spirit does hang around here. Them vigilantes will be back." Just then, he heard horses coming.

The ghost of Jenny watched from the door as Charlie and Temple stopped in the road for a last look at the cabin. The pain she felt as she knew they were leaving swept her like a brush fire. Just because she had no physical body did not immunize her against the deep, yearning hurt of her heartache. The spiritual throbbing surged in waves around the general area, but seemed to center about her arms and chest.

"*Oh, to hold them! Just once more to hold them. To feel Charlie's heart beat against my breast. If only I could be with them now, touch them. comfort them! Where was my heart when they needed me?*" The spirit of the baby hugged to her was little comfort when she remembered the needs she had overlooked. "*My son! Temple, child, don't leave.*" A moan escaped her and blended with the wind in the trees. "*I'll never hear him giggle again as his sister grips his finger in her little hand. How can they leave? How can I make them stay?"*

Jenny heard the horses coming, and fear for the safety of her loved ones gripped her. *"No! You can't stay! Go! Go!"*

As the riders came into view she recognized her murderer and anger coiled in her like a viper ready to strike. As the horses stopped in the road at the point nearest the cabin, she rose in a whirlwind as a horrible apparition to loom over the terrified men and horses. She shrieked! She screamed and cackled. The horses and riders swerved around and headed back the way they had come. Down the road, riding hard to the north, Charlie and Temple heard a mournful sigh ending in a sob which seemed to hover over them.

The ghost of Jenny watched as the threatening riders rode back the way they had come and her loved ones rode in the opposite direction.

"See, they had no choice. They couldn't stay." Pain was like a knife stabbing her heart again and again as she remembered their leaving. She shuddered in agony as the horrible skull-features showed through the ghost of beauty. The tormenting passions of love, hate, desire for revenge, battled the essence of being that hung onto the physical scene with throbbing uncertainty. The great tornado of pain soon played out and left the ghost sitting lonely as before, wondering at a fate that left her enduring torment. *"But Temple. Will he ever come back?"* She answered herself, *"No. Sooner or later he would recognize that man's voice. Then his life would be in danger too."* Her spirit floated to the waterhole again. With a last wail she asked, *"Is there no bottom to this well of loneliness?"* as she disappeared into the chill water of the McDow Hole.

"Manners that seemed almost too curious and fantastic for belief he loved to trace to their hidden sources. To unravel a tangle in the very soul of things—and to release a suffering human soul in the process—was with him a veritable passion. And the knots he untied were, indeed, often passing strange."

—ALGERNON BLACKWOOD
Ancient Sorceries

CHAPTER VI

Samuel Keith

With his short legs and long thick body, Sam Keith was a bear of a man. When he removed his once grey felt hat to wipe the sweat from his face and head, his receding hairline exposed a high slick forehead, several shades lighter than his weather-beaten face and calloused hands. Checking his cows in the lower pasture gave him the opportunity to stop by the McDow Hole and cool off a bit on the long summer days. His old boots were cracked and scuffed. As he knelt, with great difficulty, to drink from the flowing creek, he exposed holes almost through the soles of his boots and an expertly applied patch on the seat of his pants.

"Seems like the ground keeps gittin' farther and farther away every year," he muttered as he wiped the excess water from his lips with the back of his hand. His big stomach strained at the waistband of his pants and the suspenders stretched tight with the effort of bending to drink and rising afterward. His denim shirt had a few spots on the front where his cud of tobacco had leaked. "I know I ain't growed taller, so I guess I must have more to bend over." He rubbed his bulging stomach with some satisfaction, not begrudging himself a bite of good food. "Reckon I could carry myself one of them little expanding cups like Sally carries in her purse. Now wouldn't that be something." As people do who spend much time alone, Sam had learned the comfort of talking to himself. He didn't do it often, but was unashamed to be caught at it. The truth of the matter is, the one who usually caught him at it—his wife Sally—talked to herself, too.

"Real purty place here. Mighty restful." Thinking of the ghost of Jenny that was supposed to have staked a claim on the area around the McDow Hole and Papworth cabin, Sam wondered where that apparition was.

"Wonder why she don't come when I'm here?" he asked himself. "It's not like I was sneaking around trying to fool her none."

He stood a minute wondering at the feeling that he was being watched, but when he turned around to see who was staring, he saw no one. Not even a bird broke the silence. It seemed as if all nature held its breath, waiting for something.

Jenny had appeared to him only once. That was the time when he came with Chester Brownlow to the little field Charlie had managed to clear. Chester claimed that Charlie had a plow around there somewhere that belonged to him.

"Well, Chester, reckon it wouldn't hurt none for you to go look," he told Chester that morning when Chester came by his house.

"Hell, Sam, I ain't goin' there by myself. Somebody might see me and accuse me of stealing. I'm an honest man, but I know how these stories get started. Some no-good waggin' tongue would be bound to say I'd got no business there."

"Now, Chester, who'd tell a story like that? Jenny sure ain't gonna talk none," Sam teased.

"It ain't that, Sam Keith. I ain't scared of no danged woman, dead or alive. But you know the place, and where Charlie likely put my plow," said Chester.

True, Sam had known the place because he had been a good neighbor, helping Charlie when he could and advising because he was older and more experienced.

"Heck, Charlie and Jenny were almost like our own kids," Sam said to himself as he remembered Chester's coming in search of the plow. "Bet Charlie never even had his old plow."

After looking over every inch of the field and around the cabin in search of the plow, Sam and Chester stood under the big live oak that sheltered the cabin from the hot sun surveying the place to see if they had missed a likely spot. A mockingbird on an overhead limb fussed at the two for disturbing his peace. The grass had grown high between the cabin and the creek since nobody had lived there for awhile, but Sam had permission to put his cows up there to graze when he needed extra pasture. He thought to himself that he should probably put about four cows in next week to give the little patch next to his own house a rest. Then he turned his attention back to Chester and the plow.

"Are you sure Charlie had it?" Sam asked.

"Course I'm sure. I lent it to him, didn't I? I always try to be neighborly. Some folks sure take advantage of a good heart."

Sam's opinion of Chester wasn't all that good. He had loaned tools to Chester more than once, and like as not, when they were returned they'd be broken. Many times he had to go to Chester's to collect what he'd lent because Chester was too lazy to bother bringing it back. Sam recalled the time he went to retrieve an axe Chester had borrowed and found Katherine Brownlow using it to cut wood for the cook stove. She was embarrassed because she didn't know the axe belonged to Sam. She'd broken the handle out of theirs and thought Chester had taken it to town and got a new handle as she had asked him.

"Well, now, Chester, we've looked all over the place and not a plow of any kind in sight, much less a bull-tongue plow."

"That no-good horse thief probably sold it with his other stuff when he left the country like a blamed outlaw. I never should have trusted a man who would let his wife lead him around like a dumb ox. That woman was a hussy," Chester said, spitting out a stream of tobacco juice.

Sam started to protest, "Now see here…" when he saw Chester's eyes widen until they were about to pop.

"What in damnation!" Chester said and covered his face with his hands.

From the door of the cabin came a yowl that split the air—loud enough to scare the Devil himself! Then SHE came through the door, slowly, hideously. The burning eyes pinned both men to the tree. There was no escape from the menacing figure draped in dirty, ragged clothing. Her mummy-like face grinned mockingly at Chester and a bony finger seemed to stretch as she pointed at him. Then she began to laugh, and the odor of her breath, putrid and hot, swept over them.

Chester screamed, "Stop her! Stop her! That hellcat's coming to get me."

Jenny stopped for a minute, like a cat playing with a mouse it had caught, coaxing it to run again. Then she began to grow, gathering strength and sustenance from a spiraling column of air like a giant whirlwind, yet never losing the shape and appearance of a woman.

Chester didn't need any coaxing and neither did Sam. They

ran to the creek, crossed the shallows, and fled toward Sam's house.

Later, when he told Sally about the ghost he and Chester had seen, she got excited and asked him over and over about her, but Sam had very few answers for her many questions. All he could say was, "I guess that foul mouth of Chester's just offended her."

After that frightful day, Sam was reluctant to go near the McDow Hole, but fright or no fright, ghost or no ghost, he had no choice. The hot dry summer made it necessary to return to the spring-fed water hole—the place where Jenny's spirit was most likely to appear.

On one occasion when he had filled a barrel at the water hole and loaded it onto his wagon, Sam lay down to rest against the huge pecan tree for just a few minutes before going back to his house.

Sam woke with a start. His first thought was that Jenny had found him again, when in truth Jenny had been watching him peacefully. As Doc rode up, she hovered nearby, carefully remaining invisible to them both. It seemed odd to her that she could share their peace. Usually when someone dared to enter her domain she did not hesitate to exert her power to frighten. But with these two friends, she found herself willing to remain unseen and share the mood of the atmosphere.

"Sorry I woke you, Sam. You looked so comfortable I almost rode on by," said Doc.

"Yep, well. Guess I did doze off. Seems easy to do these warm evenings." Sam struggled a little to get to his feet.

"Don't get up. I'll just join you, if you don't mind." Doc sat so that he could see the creek and Sam at the same time. He always liked to look at the person he was talking to.

"Real nice here with that little west breeze. Jest needed somebody to pass the time of day. You been out visiting the sick, Doc?"

"Smith boy has the measles," said Doc. Doctor Jed Eakins made it a point to come by the McDow Hole when he could. And not just because it was the prettiest place on the creek...the many stories he'd heard about the Papworths and their tragedies made him curious about the ghost.

"I've been wanting to ask you something, Sam. You and Sally were the ones who found Jenny when she was killed, weren't you? How do you reckon she died?"

"Yeah, she and the kids had been staying nights at our house while Charlie went off to Georgia. For some reason they didn't come that night and Sally and me was kinda worried. Wish to God we had come to see about her that night instead of waiting till morning. We might could'a saved her," Sam said, shaking his head.

Doc just nodded without saying anything. He knew from experience all about those back thoughts and the hunger to do things over again and get them right next time. Never could be. Just as well. Something else to regret. He knew how hard it was to go on living with decisions once they were made. He knew how hard it was not to relive events...how hard it was to force your mind into different pursuits.

"You know she didn't always come at the same time. Sometimes it would be good dark, and that night we kept thinking she was just delayed. Anyhow, we waited till daylight to come over and check. Reckon we couldn't have saved Jenny anyway. From the looks of her, she'd been hit a number of times.

There was blood on her face from a cut in the cheek. Her nose was broken and bloody. But what killed her was the choking. Her neck was blue and you could see the marks where his hands had pressed the life out of her." Even now, after all this time, Sam had a hard time talking about it.

"The baby was over against the wall, dead. It had a big ugly place on its poor little face and the back of her head was caved in. Horrible…it was just horrible. My Sally ain't a hysterical woman, thank God. But she turned white as a sheet, ran outside and up-chucked before she could come back in. We was about to decide there wasn't nothin' to do but go to Alexander and get the sheriff, when we heard something. It was a little sobbing noise, like kids do when they cry theirselves to sleep. Sally looked behind the bed and found Temple. We put him in the buggy with us and I dropped him and Sally off at home before going on to Alexander."

"Sam, I know how you must have felt." Doc was remembering the scene when he found Florence after she had been beaten and raped. He had to ask. "Was she raped, do you think?"

"Well, me and Sally talked about it. She was better at picturing what happened than I was. The room was all tore up. You could see there had been a real fight; the table was turned over, things was scattered everywhere. The gun was off the rack and had been fired, but the shot had hit the door. We don't think anyone was hit. Sally says whoever it was had tried to rape her, but she fought so hard he must of got mad and choked her. Maybe she's the one that got the gun and shot."

"What about her clothes?"

"They was all torn and half off. Sally says she must have fought him terrible hard, especially when he threatened to hurt the baby. 'Course we didn't have a doctor to examine her.

Weren't none here then. But the way her body was layin'—sorta thrown against the table and other things, me and Sally decided he intended to rape her but killed her instead," Sam said.

"What about Temple? Could he tell you who did it?"

"Poor kid. He was so scared—and sick too. I guess he was asleep when the man or men came, and woke up during the fight and just hid himself behind the bed. He couldn't tell us anything about it. It must have happened after dark. Looked like the lamp had been lit, but it wasn't burning when we got there and it was almost full of oil. Guess the little tyke was lucky that the men didn't see him."

"He didn't ever say anything about it?"

"All he told Sally was that he had a sore throat. That may be why they stayed home that night," said Sam.

"And you never did find out who killed her?" asked Doc.

"Never did. The story got around that Indians done it, but I never believed that. We ain't had no mean Indians in these parts fer several years now. Mind you, when we first come to Erath County they was a few renegades came through ever once in a while. Mostly they was ones the vigilantes had stirred up. Me and Charlie had some good Indian friends that visited ever so often...Caddos. Back several years ago when the reservations were moved to Oklahoma, a few of them managed to get back to their farms in parts south of here. Baylor and his vigilantes were the cause of them being moved in the first place. These here usually brought some seed or vegetables to trade with us. You know that calico corn I got that makes such good cornmeal? Running Deer brought me the seed for that. No, it weren't no Indian done that to Jenny. That was a mean, worthless white bastard. And I'll bet money on it."

Sam stretched and looked up with a sense of unease. He felt

like everything stopped and waited. His skin prickled. Doc, too, felt the sudden heaviness of the air—a hush of expectancy, as he looked toward the creek.

"Look, Sam! What's that down there by the water?"

"Well, I swan! That do look like Jenny!"

The figure of a woman was walking by the edge of the water along the deep end of the hole. Though her skirts looked thin and filmy, they didn't blow in the breeze. The figure turned toward the two men and nodded with a sense of recognition, then turned toward the sunset and stood a moment, just before she stepped onto the water and vanished.

Sam struggled to his feet and he and Doc stood to watch.

"Now don't that beat all! If you wasn't here to tell me otherwise, I'd think I was dreaming," Sam said.

"Lord, yes, we both saw her. Did it look like Jenny?"

"Not only looked like her, it was her!" said Sam. "I've seen her dressed in that Sunday dress many times."

"Think about it, Sam. That was not the horrible creature we've heard about when others saw her."

"You're right, Doc. That was the beautiful woman Jenny rightly was. Why do you suppose we saw one thing and them others saw something else?"

CHAPTER VII

Dinner on the Ground

It was Sunday and time for dinner-on-the-ground at the Baptist church in Alexander. Several men were relaxing in the shade of the trees, after the exertion of getting planks laid across the sawhorses for the table. The women unloaded wonders of fried chicken, pound cakes, cream pies, potato salads and nameless masterpieces from baskets and boxes that husbands had brought to the table from wagons. Looking at each addition and commenting to each other about the makings, the women also caught up on the news. They asked about every absent family and accounted for the children playing ante-over with a string ball over the church house. They also half listened to the tales the men were telling.

"Did you hear 'bout the vigilante raid over near Hico?" asked Franklin.

"Don't guess I did, Franklin. Who'd they get this time?" asked Sam.

"Well, the depot agent said after a train robbery near Grapevine last Saturday night the hooded plague decided to catch the thieves. Don't know where they got their information or how good it was, but they rounded up six men and hanged them. One man managed to escape when the horse of a vigilante carrying a torch reared and threw the rider. He took off through the underbrush and hid where they couldn't find him in all the commotion. Mr. Green, ticket man at the depot, said the escapee bought a train ticket next day to go to Austin and complain about the vigilantes."

"High time someone put a stop to them bastards," said Franklin.

"You're right about that," agreed Sam Keith as he chose a stick for whittling.

After a few more tales about the vigilantes, the general subject for both groups gradually turned to sightings of Jenny, the ghost that haunted the McDow Hole on Green's Creek.

Doc Eakins seemed to be the chief authority on the subject, though he was a late comer who never knew the Papworths. He seemed to have made kind of a study about Jenny since he came to the area. And he dearly loved to be center stage and tell stories. With his doctoring satchel tied behind his saddle, he had been to every family in the area to doctor a bit and help with birthings, though the women helped each other, too. Usually, babies didn't wait until Doc could be located and travel several miles on horseback. The nearest neighbor woman was summoned and Doc came later to check on the mother and child.

The same sort of after-care occurred many times at death, too. But the doctor's usual rounds revealed needs he could serve, and he was a comforting soul. He seemed to know when hidden pain gnawed, and when a man or woman needed words of comfort or nods of understanding. Doc was a big man with amazing dexterity and tenderness in fingers as big around as sausages. He could gently feel broken bones, and while saying soothing words to shocked patients, he could coax muscles and bones to harmonize. Before the patient was aware, he had a splint and bandages in place.

With his big black hat pulled down to protect deep grey eyes under bushy eyebrows, the doctor was recognized from as far away as the hills and trees would allow vision, as anxious family members watched. But his twelve years of city practice and eight years of riding herd over farm families had seemed to make time accumulate quickly.

Especially the last four years, since Florence, his wife, had died, Doc felt old. His big body had begun to protest when he pulled himself up into the saddle. His knee and hip joints had to be coaxed into working when he rolled out of bed, and he swallowed more baking soda to soothe his acid stomach than Florence had used in baking.

Believing in ghosts or not believing in ghosts was not really the question people asked themselves when they talked of Jenny. Something haunted that little cabin and surroundings. Too many people had encountered Jenny to make it a trick of the imagination. Of course, some folks liked to invent topics of conversation with themselves center stage, but enough real experiences happened to supply ordinary gatherings with interesting talk. Some brave souls went to the haunting grounds especially to see if Jenny would appear, but many had to go to that hole of water in the summer time to haul water. Springs kept water there even when the rest of the creek was dry. Thirsty people seemed grateful that Jenny made no objection to their getting water. She didn't threaten, or even appear most of the time when people went there from need, but when she did appear, she made a lasting impression.

Ghosts and spirits didn't seem unreasonable to Doc. He never told anyone about how often in the period of his deep grief after Florence died that he saw her, or thought he saw her, in her accustomed places. He knew from sharing other's griefs that it was not uncommon for the grieving one to occasionally feel the presence of the dead one, or even to think they saw them. But he never expected to experience the phenomenon with such intensity. So often when he rode up to the home stable about sundown, he'd see Florence standing on the back porch watching for him. If he came a little earlier, he'd see her out feeding the chickens and hear them talking to her. His yearnings had pictured her there so many times and so vividly. Not until too late did he realize how lonesome she must have been on those long days when he was out making rounds. She had always been waiting for him. She hadn't complained, and until he experienced the ache, he hadn't realized how her life was built around him. Sometimes, after her death, her image and the feeling of her presence was so profound that he caught himself talking to her. So maybe she did stay around for awhile. Maybe she was there, helping him to adjust to a life without her. Perhaps she knew he needed time to accept the reality of death. Though he had seen the effect on others, not until he lost Florence had he lost a part of himself.

Doc remembered how he had avoided inviting anyone into his house those first days and weeks after the funeral. Good neighbors came with food and condolences. Usually, he met them on the porch and accepted their tokens of caring there. For a long time, he preferred being alone with his memories. After all, what would folks think if they came in and found him sitting beside an empty chair talking to the lonesome air? Even if she were visible to him, he was sure others would not see her.

Gradually, he saw her less and less, and the loneliness crowded him more and more. His needs changed. He stayed away from home as much as he could, but her presence had helped him to adjust. How could you explain things like that to anyone, he wondered as he sat under the trees in the church yard. Who would trust a doctor who saw someone who was not there? Best to just keep his mouth shut, he told himself again.

There was one person he used to talk to a little, Bill Atchison. Bill came to the area about five years before, looking for something— peace, perhaps. Anyway, he was a troubled man who mostly kept to himself. He was a cabinet maker by trade, but there wasn't much call for cabinets in and around Alexander. Women considered themselves lucky when they had those convenient free-standing cabinets with a bin for flour and a drawer for flatware, as well as some shelves with doors to protect the supplies. Sure beat a shelf and box against a dirt wall. So Bill filled a need folks couldn't avoid. He became the coffin maker. Not wanting to live close to others, but needing to be near enough for people to come for his wares, he looked for just the right place. Though people warned him about Jenny, he had decided to stay in the Papworth cabin just the same. Said he wasn't afraid of ghosts, except for the personal ones he brought with him.

Doc got into the habit of stopping by to talk, or to listen to Bill play the fiddle. Sometimes Bill would be drunk for several days at a time, but other times he was good company. He had tried to leave his memories behind when he came to Texas, but they came, too. No one ever knew where he came from, or what—or who—he was running away from. He just appeared and blended with other brave settlers who may have had things in their past which wouldn't bear daylight.

That Sunday, Doc had the floor. He enjoyed refreshing memories and spinning yarns. "You all remember Bill Atchison? Anyone who ever saw him would remember Bill. I used to visit with him some evenings. He was a real eye-catcher, wasn't he? Remember that long handle-bar mustache? Why he had a lot more hair on his face than on his shiny head. Big man. Ruddy complexion, and a funny thing about that bald head, you could see his pulse beating clear as anything. Guess most people wouldn't notice a thing like that, but I did.

"Bill looked like a party man, but he never went to socials— only went to church occasionally. If it hadn't been for his drinking he could probably have been successful in the city. Reckon that's why he came way out here, though. Bill had enough of city ways."

"Weren't he the one that made all them coffins? I remember hearing him hammering away many nights when I rode past. When someone died sudden like, or got hisself killed, Bill would work all night to finish his coffin," said Franklin as he whittled himself a toothpick.

Franklin was a long drink of water. He was tall and skinny, with weathered lines fanning out from a big hooked nose on his sun darkened face. He never looked for trouble, took his time making up his mind, but a neighbor in need could count on Franklin to help if it was in his power. He farmed a few acres beyond the McDow Hole and did some surveying for the state when he was needed.

"Yep, that was him, Franklin. I guess you could say Bill and me were partners." Doc continued. "When a body was too sick for me to help them, Bill took over. Whenever someone had been sick awhile, Bill would ask me if he should start a box. He took pride in having the coffin done before the dying, if he had a little warning. He always called 'em boxes. That's all they are, really. Just a box made to fit. Nothing fancy like those ruffled, satin-lined ones in the big funeral parlors in Fort Worth. But then, folks 'round here never lived in fancy houses while they were alive. Little late to start wanting frills after you're dead, I guess. Did you ever hear Bill play the fiddle?"

"I heard him sometimes," said Sam Keith. "I 'member one time in particular. It was 'bout sundown one evening when I was out hunting that blamed ole one-eared cow of mine over in the pasture towards Jenny's cabin. That cow's so dumb she won't come in with the rest, even when her calf's bawling his head off. I think the timber wolf that got her ear got her brains, too. Well, I heard Bill playing. It was such a—I don't know—a lonesome sound, mournful but purty, too. I sat down and listened for awhile," said Sam Keith.

"Yeah, he could make lonesome music that would wring tears from the eye of a tater. He'd sit on a stool in the middle of the floor, plant his feet firmly in front of him like he was afraid of falling off the stool, tuck his violin under his chin and pause. Guess he was making a selection out of his head, but seemed like he was listening for a request. You know, many folks can play the fiddle well enough to dance by, but guess you have to call it a violin when a man makes the air come alive with moods and music like Bill could.

"Sometimes he played soft and dreamy, and my eyes would grow heavy—but I didn't go to sleep. Like as not, I'd feel like I was walking on bottomless clouds. Other times he could play the bugs off the turnip vines. More often than not, though, Bill played sad music, like Sam said. That violin spoke of broken hearts and heart breakers. It was lonesome and sad, and made a lump come in my throat. Tears would come in Bill's eyes, too, and you could tell his heart was talking through those strings." Doc stopped to take a sip of coffee from his tin cup.

"He could play happy, too. Made me want to dance sometimes, and I didn't even dance much with Florence—wish I had done more, though. Wouldn't have hurt me to have taken her dancing occasionally when they had dances at the neighbors' houses. She was always wanting to go when we was younger. Guess she gave up trying to persuade me, cause she quit asking. Anyway, Bill could make you want to dance." Doc ducked his head to hide the surge of feeling.

"Reckon Jenny wanted to dance when she heard him? Did he ever say anything about seeing the ghost?" asked Keith.

"Yeah, I wonder if he did. That ghost first appeared about six months after Jenny died, and was seen pretty often just before Bill moved in the Papworth cabin," said Franklin.

"Well, sir, I nearly always asked him about that," said Doc. "He told me once that she'd been around a time or two. He said one night he waked up and someone, Jenny I guess, was sobbing like her heart was broken. At first he thought it was a dream, but he lay there after he was sure he was awake and the crying went on and on. It was like she was trying to be quiet, but couldn't. Bill said he didn't quite know whether to slip out of bed and investigate, or to cover his head and wait for morning. A one-room cabin is mighty little with a crying woman, let alone the crying ghost of one. Finally he got up enough nerve to roll out of bed on the back side and light a glut. Nobody was there! He said it sounded like, before he got up, she was sitting on a stool there by the table sobbing something awful. But he couldn't see her and the crying stopped soon as he got out of bed."

"I tell you fer sure, Doc, I'd 've been the one that left. And I would've done it at top speed. I ain't scared of much human, but I don't hold much in common with haints." Franklin was telling the truth. He wasn't afraid of anyone he had met. He had surveyed all over the county, even when the Comanches were raiding.

"Yes, sir," agreed Sam Keith, "that one time would have been enough for me to be so near to her. What do you 'spose made her so unhappy?"

"Well, now. I don't think she ever was happy, was she, Sam? Course, I never knew the lady when she was alive. Guess they moved here while I was still in Fort Worth. But from stories I've heard, she wasn't too happy with life here. She always talked about the fine things of Georgia, and wanted to go back there," said Doc.

"Yeah, that's right. We were their closest neighbors, and she came riding over to our house on that mare lots of times. My wife helped her when their baby was born, and we was the ones that missed her after the murder. But I think you're right. She just never did let herself be one of us," said Sam Keith.

"Did you and Bill ever talk about what he thought she was crying fer, Doc?" asked Franklin.

"Bill had some ideas. He thought maybe that was about the time the ghost of the baby disappeared. Maybe even a spirit feels a loss like that."

"Could be. At first when anyone seen her she had that baby held real close. But lately, no one has mentioned the baby—and she seems more fierce than ever," said Sam.

"Bill did tell about seeing her one time when she had the baby with her. Seems it was along about midnight one time in the summer. Bill said he usually slept with the door open in the summer because it was so blamed hot in that shut-up cabin. He also did his cooking on the outside in the summer so as not to get the place all heated up."

"Yeah, we tried that, too. But Millie likes her cookstove. Now that we got it, Millie does all the cooking for the day early in the morning so's the cabin can cool off a mite before bedtime. But tell us about Bill and the ghost. I've always been curious about how he died," said Franklin.

"Well, sir, Bill said for some reason he shut the door that night. Oh, it was hot all right, but he felt like he needed to shut the door. So about midnight he was trying to sleep in the hot stuffy cabin, and had just dozed off when he was awakened by something. Took him a few minutes to decide what woke him, then he heard a soft knock at the door. Thinking it was me or some traveler, he went to see. He opened the door and was almost knocked down by a rush of real cold wind. But he held the door and rubbed his eyes before he could see well in the dark. There in the white moonlight was Jenny with her babe in her arms! That hideous grinning, mummy-like face peered up at him! He slammed the door and pushed the bolt home. Then, trembling, he got back in bed—but not to sleep. Telling me about it a couple of days later he was puzzled because she looked so distressed and even bothered to knock at the door. He said other times she had just floated through the shut door, but she wasn't so sorrowful those other times."

"Can a feller be scared to death, Doc? Is that what happened to Bill? You're the one found him. Did he die of fear?" Keith was asking the question everybody had wondered about .

"Well, sir, I just don't know. Didn't seem to be any other reason for him to die. He wasn't sick the day before, and there was no evidence of trauma. When we found him he was just lying there on the floor. No sign of struggle in the cabin."

"Remember I saw him, too, Doc," said Sam. "He had the most horrified look on his face. He shore looked scared."

"You're right about the look. It could have been caused by pain. Sometimes when pain hits suddenly it really messes up a face. But then I don't rightly know. The funny thing about his death was not to be seen about the body though."

"No? What was that, Doc?" asked Franklin.

"Well, sir. Bill had made himself a box just the day he died! I noticed the fresh cedar smell the minute I walked in the cabin. Most boxes he just made of pine or the native oak. But that one balanced on the table, all smoothed and polished, was made of cedar—and it had W. C. Atchison carved on the end."

"Do tell. You mean he made it that very day?" Sam knew it was true, but liked for Doc to tell his version.

"Yes, sir. I swear it was not there, nor anywhere else about the place on the day before when Bill and I had a long visit. Bill made his box the day he died that night. Made it to fit and made it pretty."

"Avaunt! and quit my sight! Let the earth hide thee!
Thy bones are marrowless, thy blood is cold,
Thou hast no speculation in those eyes
Which thou dost glare with!"

—SHAKESPEARE
Macbeth

CHAPTER VIII

Doc's Troubles

It had been a long difficult delivery, and heart breaking, because Doc was unable to save the baby. On his way home, about mid-day, he stopped at the McDow Hole to rest a minute. The muscles in his face sagged with weariness as he took off his old black hat and mopped the sweat from his forehead with his sleeve, but he couldn't wipe the depression from his eyes. He washed the smell of alcohol from his hands and washed his face in the cool water, rubbing some onto his greying blonde hair. The breeze on the wet head felt wonderful. He crossed the creek at the shallow crossing just above the hole, wading, never mind his old boots. Not much more than the soles got wet. After his horse drank his fill, Doc led him to the big pecan tree up from the east bank. Dropping the reins to let the horse graze, he was vaguely aware of the irritated caws of a dozen or so crows that he disturbed from the pecan tree. They didn't go far from their treasure, only to a willow on the edge of the creek. It was late August and the nuts were beginning to drop from their green hulls to the ground. Crows were the first to know when harvest time was come.

Doc's boots mashed some of the green hulls, releasing a sharp scent to tease the nose. Sliding wearily down to sit on the grass with his back against the rough bark of the tree, Doc sighed. Letting a bit of the tension drain away as the evaporating water cooled his head and face, he savored the bit of peace of the scene. It was like unwrapping a small treasured gift from protecting wrappings for another peek, and he wanted to claim that bit of tranquility to replace the hunger that seemed a constant companion lately.

Florence and Doc had come to Alexander from Fort Worth, running from an experience that had changed not only their lives, but their life perspectives as well. The beautiful, dark-eyed young bride with the long dark brown hair and a smile that melted hearts, would never regain her childlike joy and wonder of life after her experience in Fort Worth. She lived, but was permanently scarred by a nightmare beating and rape committed by burglars who broke into their apartment—and Doc would never be free of the hate, outrage, guilt and drive for revenge.

It hadn't been easy to leave the relative conveniences of the city for frontier life, but the city held no shred of peace for them. The move to the country was a balm for their spirits, but only the promise of peace had been achieved in the time before Florence's death. Doc pulled his thoughts from those channels with a conscious effort. He was too tired and depressed already to contend with the feelings of outrage and guilt that still crowded out the happy memories.

But feelings of helplessness, of defeat, with the death of an infant, engulfed him now as he rested under the pecan tree. If only he had the knowledge and equipment to ease the trauma of birth when complications occurred. If only he could reach patients before fever was raging and infections rampant. If only he could teach these people basic health care and nutrition. If only old superstitions did not seem to them the proper treatment for illness. If the country people only had the means to own necessities of life. The "if only's" chased each other in vicious circles in his head. He hugged the despair to himself as if it could fill his inner void. Instead, it was digging a deeper vacuum to create a greater emptiness.

Doc purposely concentrated his attention on a curious, hungry squirrel who came cautiously to share the shade with him. He watched as the squirrel found a pecan, flicked his tail, and began eating. The squirrel eyed him with distrust, but seeing no movement, began to eat hungrily, ready in an instant for a retreat.

"Hey, fellow. Found a good pecan?"

The squirrel dropped the nut when Doc spoke, but still seeing no threatening moves he soon picked it up again. The man decided to cooperate. If the squirrel was content to share the shade with him, he would try not to make sudden moves. The tired man watched as the little animal tucked the remainder of the pecan in his jaw and scampered up the tree.

Suddenly, Doc was conscious of absolute quiet. The crows were gone, the squirrel had disappeared, the other birds had vanished. The horse had stopped chomping and snorting. He might have thought himself half asleep and the apparition a dream, except that he was still too tired and tense to sleep, and felt his heart skip a beat as the very atmosphere waited expectantly. Slowly, as he stared toward the creek, a pillar of fog, or mist, seemed to rise from the ground. The formless cloud seemed to gather in upon itself, gaining substance and shape. Doc watched as if mesmerized, not at all surprised to see a woman step toward him. He was filled with the wonder of a child when he sees a newly hatched chick. It wasn't terror he felt, but a sense of unease made him sit more erect. He felt a prickling sensation along his arms and back, as if small ants from the tree bark were crawling on him. But he didn't feel revulsion or panic—yet. Perhaps the spirit of Florence had taught him to accept the unexpected, the unexplainable, because he did accept and acknowledge a presence as a young woman with red hair walked toward him.

Jenny seemed to hesitate at first, not trusting the man, though she knew that she was immune to any hurt from human beings, now. Still, the distrust she had learned from experiences in her lifetime was yet a habit. Never had she appeared in this fashion before, controlled, curious. She felt momentarily drained of the destructive emotions that had governed her actions up to this point, but she knew that control was very precarious. She felt in Doc, a man who had earned a small measure of peace, one who consciously sought to share peace, and she was drawn to that emotion like an ant to honey.

"You must be Jenny," said Doc, only half believing.

She took a step forward, and then the dam erupted! Her control shattered! Seething emotions came flooding back. The pent-up hate and fear and resentment flamed like throwing oil on a fire. As she uttered a horrible shriek of despair the beautiful features of the woman became the heinous ones shown to others, the skeletal face with long-dead matted hair and eyes of piercing daggers. As Doc jumped to his feet in fright the body again became a pillar of fog and was sucked into the ground.

Doc ran to his frightened horse, jumped into the saddle, and didn't stop until he got home. By that time he was thinking calmly about the appearance and wondering at the transformation of feelings he saw in the ghost and reacted to himself. Disbelief made his attempt at analysis seem futile, but he had to acknowledge his own feelings.

When he got home, Doc tended to his horse and got a bucket of chicken feed for the excited rooster who flew to the top of the barnyard gate and called his flock. Lately Doc had been talking to himself regularly as he did the chores. Sometimes his remarks were addressed to Florence, though he knew her spirit was no longer around, nor would he wish it to be. She deserved to rest in peace, and he had finally come to grips with his loss of her caring comfort. Only the memories haunted the place now, so even when he addressed Florence he knew he was talking to himself—or the chickens, or dog, or horse, which was the same. Still, the sound of a voice took the edge off the loneliness.

"Chick, chick, chick. You wouldn't believe what I saw this evening, ladies. And I thought people were just telling tales, especially about the frightfulness." Hens talk back. Their hen talk was friendly and chatty, as if they were happy to hear any news at all.

The familiar motions of feeding the hens was automatic as Doc continued to listen to his own thoughts, "That was a real troubled soul I saw today. Don't know why, but that was raw emotion I saw. It was like the wailing of the Indian grandmother, Soon-Lou's this morning, only hers was the heartrending sound of sorrow. Jenny's wail wasn't sorrow, but it was pulled from the heart like Soon-Lou's."

Doc thought of how startled he was, and of the fright of George Sikes when his mother-in-law saw the lifeless little baby and began to moan. "I guess that Indian death wail was as strange to George as it was to me, even though she had lived with him and Ruth Ann for several years. I reckon I looked just as scared when Jenny shrieked as George did this morning."

Although he continued to think of the experience for several days, Doc was not yet ready to tell about it. Still he found himself drawn to the McDow Hole.

"I just think I could communicate with her some way. Poor thing. She didn't have the baby with her today. Reckon its soul has gone on to heaven. The Lord said to let them come. Guess that little infant of George's and Jenny's baby are safe and happy, though their leaving brought lots of grief here," Doc mused. He determined to go by the McDow Hole the next day.

Doc's first stop the next morning was the saloon to see if any messages had been left for him, and to have a cup of coffee with Jake. In the daytime the place was more like a cafe with red checkered cloths on the tables and the smell of cooking and clatter of dishes coming from the back. It was the communication center for the town of Alexander. Jake, wearing a once white duck apron to protect the fancy pants he wore for bartending, served breakfast and lunch before the drinking crowd came in.

Jake, with his sharp eyes and hook nose holding wireframed glasses, worn low enough that he could look over them for a longer focus by ducking his head a little, searched for news like a long legged crane searched for and stabbed fish in the nearby tank. In fact, his long legs and arms added to the similarity. If anyone knew about what went on, day or night, it was the friendly barkeep. He kept a Mexican man busy in the kitchen cooking and cleaning up nights. Other than that, Jake ran the place himself, and wasn't over-worked.

"'Bout time you got here, Doc," said Jake wiping his hands on his apron as he walked around from behind the bar. "We was about to decide to go to your house and get you. This young man," he nodded his head toward a man slumped in a chair, leaning on a table, "came in 'bout an hour ago with a hurt leg. His name's Robert Key."

"Howdy, Robert," Doc held out his hand as he walked toward Robert. Robert raised his head and looked with bleary eyes at the doctor. "Let's see that leg, now," said Doc, noting the signs of pain and distress in the young face. "Guess you'll have to drop your pants. Can't pull them up that high." He helped Robert to his feet.

Robert was a husky young fellow with dark shaggy hair and brown eyes. He looked like he might be trying to grow a mustache, except that he didn't have many whiskers to work with. The sour smell of night-after liquor and no bath clung to him as he struggled to pull his pants down, propping unsteadily on the chair for support.

The pain was too intense for him to worry about modesty. Blood had dried, pasting the pants to the leg. As Doc gave a jerk to pull them loose and expose the wound, Robert dropped limply into the chair, and his head went on to land on the checkered cloth of the table. He had fainted, and would have slid out of the chair if Jake hadn't caught him by the shoulders and held him in it.

"Guess that's a bullet wound, Jake," said Doc, taking advantage of the faint to probe. "Don't look so bad. Here's where it went in and here's where it came out. Didn't hit a bone, but needs cleaning. Wonder where he was when he got shot."

"He said a bunch of them was down at the ghost hole last night. Guess things got a little exciting," said Jake, smiling as he thought about what a good story it would make.

Robert was coming to, but he groaned with pain. "Damn! That hurts," he said, rolling his eyes up in a pleading fashion.

"Jake, fetch my bag off the saddle out there. Guess I better clean this thing a bit. How'd you get here, Robert? You couldn't have walked from the ghost hole with this wound. Don't tell me Jenny's carrying a gun these days."

"No, sir. I didn't walk. Frank brought me on his horse. Took awhile with both of us on him. My horse ran off during the ruckus," said Robert.

"Tell me about it, son. Try to remember the whole thing." Doc was beginning the clean-up job and wanted to get Robert's mind off the hurt.

"'Bout five of us buddies wanted to know what all the ghost talk was about. Ouch! Doc. Do you have to dig so deep?"

"Hell, Robert. I'm just putting some novocain in here. Pretty soon you won't even know you've got a leg. Did you see Jenny?" Somehow Doc didn't want to call her "the ghost." For him, she had a definite identity, a character, since he had spent so much time thinking about her. He'd about decided to do some investigating to find what really happened to her to make her so fierce and unhappy.

"We sure did! And we didn't even go in the cabin." Robert might not have been so sure if his leg didn't hurt so bad. But that was no imagination. "We just built a little fire down there on the creek bank and were settin' there talking."

"What was you jawing about?" asked Jake, wanting to get all the particulars to make his own story, and helping Doc keep Robert's mind off his leg.

"Well, sir, the moon was out purty, and you could see hundreds of stars. The fire made a good smell. It was real peaceful-like. Seth had a jug of cider we was passing around and we was talking about what people said about that ghost. Must've been right smart after three o'clock when it happened, 'cause we didn't decide to go there until late."

"Just what happened, Robert?" asked Doc.

"Damned if I know. The fire had burned down to coals, 'cause we uz thinking about going home, when all of a sudden this here woman jest sorta floated up with the smoke out of the fire! She's a horrible creature! Looked like she'd been dead and buried for years, but she just floated up, and up!" Robert shuddered as he remembered. "She was taller than a good sized tree, just towering over us with red coals of fire for eyes and matted red hair, and she sorta swayed over us." When Robert swayed in his chair Jake held him upright again.

"Watch out, boy! You'll fall outen that chair, yet," said Jake.

"It was a warm night and a warm fire, but I shivered as cold wind and a rotten odor hit me," remembered Robert. "Then she began to laugh! It was a horrible cackle, sort of a witch's laugh!"

"Where'd the shot come from, Robert?" asked Jake.

"Well, sir, you know, someone—I don't rightly know which one—pulled his gun and shot at that ghost! Then all hell broke loose! Everybody started shooting and running. My horse ran away." Robert shook his head in wonder. "I reckon he's home by now. It was lucky fer me that Frank had trouble catching his horse, cause I kept yelling at him after the others were gone. I ran a few steps and fell. By then he got brave enough to stoop and help me on behind. I sure thought I was going to have to spend the night with that ghost."

Just as Doc was putting the bandage on, Rube Burr came in and Robert had to tell the story all over again. With no longer any pain in the wound to disturb his concentration, the story was better the second time Robert told it.

"Hell, you don't really think you saw a ghost, do you? Likely it was something out of that jug ya'll were passing." Rube looked like someone who had all the answers, no matter what the questions were. He straightened the collar on his plaid shirt and gave his pants a hitch. Rube would have looked like a regular farmer, except that his boots were always shined. He was a wiry little man, and if he was not wearing his gun, it was handy in his saddle bag. He usually didn't wear it into the saloon because he knew Jake didn't approve—not that he really cared who approved of him, he just tried to cooperate when it suited him.

"But all five of us saw the same thing!" Robert said.

"Must of been somebody hiding down there to scare you boys. Ain't no such thing as ghosts."

"Well, Rube, if it was somebody laying to scare them, they had to be real brave. Old Kit had a forty-five and a couple of the others had guns. Mix a little liquor with that and only a fool would try to scare them in the dark," said Jake.

"That don't make no difference. I won't believe in no ghost. If I can't reach out my hand and touch it, it ain't there," said Rube.

Doc just listened, putting aside his plan to go to the McDow that day. He wanted to go when Jenny was calmer. He wanted to get to know her in peace.

Jake got a gleam in his eye as he thought of a plan.

"Hey, Rube. Bet you won't stay down at that cabin all night," he said.

Rube was willing to make a little wager. "I'll bet you a hundred dollars I will."

Jake knew that Rube had money from some source, because just last weekend he had paid Ben Green a twenty-dollar gold piece for the use of his fast little filly. Nobody with judgment went around paying like that. Five dollars would have been the going price. Besides, it was a marvel to Jake how little people really knew about the Burr brothers. They had moved onto a farm in the community and were pretty good farmers, but they sure did go to Fort Worth often, two or three weekends in a row, sometimes. "Me and Doc'll call that, by George. We could use a little extra money, couldn't we, Doc?" Jake looked at his friend for agreement.

"Well, now, guess we'd have to put a few conditions on the bet, but I'm willing. If I can't dig up $50 I guess I could do like some of my patients and pay you in eggs or pigs, or something, couldn't I Jake?" Doc grinned. He was just as sure as Jake that the money was in the bag.

"I don't trust you guys to hold the money. Who can we get to hold the bet?" asked Rube.

"How 'bout the ticket agent down to the depot. He's got 'bout the only safe round here," Jake said.

"All right, boys. On one condition. My brother Jim goes with me," said Rube.

"We don't object to that, do we Doc? Seems fair that we go down there with you and bring your horses back to town so's we can be sure you really stay." Jake was thinking ahead and making plans, though he was doubtful whether Rube and Jim would show up that evening with the money.

"This unbroken success he attributed solely to the observance of his lifelong motto: The human brain needs only to become fully aware of its powers to conquer even the elements."

—CARL STEPHENSON
Leiningen Versus the Ants

CHAPTER IX

Rube and Jim Burr

Jake's fingers were itching to get hold of the Burrs' hundred dollars, but Doc was really surprised when the brothers showed up about four o'clock that afternoon with their money in hand. It was easy to see why Rube wanted brother Jim with him. Jim was quite an enlargement of the first brother, very similar in general appearance but must have been six-foot-six in his stocking feet. The boots showing beneath too-short pants were gleaming. His long legs took two strides to three of the other men as they walked to the depot to deposit their bets with the station master.

"Guess Rube was really hungry for excitement when he made this bet with you boys. Me and him've got plenty to do out on the farm, but it don't take much to distract him from farm work," said Jim.

"Maybe Jake is figgering on going to meet Jenny himself and wants you'all to see if it's safe first," said Doc.

They talked of Robert and the other boys' experience, and several other sightings.

Jim laughed, "Doc, when you and Jake give your money to Mr. Carson at the depot, you may as well kiss it goodbye. Ain't no haint gonna scare me and Rube. We don't scare much."

They watched the money as it was tucked safely away and went back to the saloon to get the horses. Jake told Manuel to watch the saloon and they headed for the Papworth cabin down on Green's Creek.

Rube and Jim, joking and planning how they were going to get the best night's sleep of their lives, took their bed rolls from their saddles and waved as they were left there in the cabin yard.

Next morning Doc went to the saloon early so that he and Jake could take their horses to the Burr brothers, but when they went to the stable to get them, Jim and Rube had already picked them up. They had walked in about daylight, awakened the stable owner and hit the trail for home.

Doc and Jake wondered if the money was theirs to pick up.

"We may never know what happened, Doc. Them two likely won't tell if they got scared," said Jake.

"Maybe not, Jake. They'll be in for some funning if they show, you can bet."

In spite of the teasing they knew they would get, Rube and Jim showed up at the saloon that evening. Knowing that every-body already knew of their early morning walk, they decided they had a tale worth telling, even if they did have to eat crow and change their tune about ghosts. As the men, including Doc, gathered around to hear the latest, Rube, the bigger talker of the two was ready. First, however, he set his drink on the bar and stooped over to wipe the toe of his boot, because somebody jostled his elbow and made him spill a bit of his liquor. Taking a handkerchief out of his pocket he carefully shined the spot, folded his handkerchief just so again and placed it neatly in his pocket. Rube always took time for the little niceties—or was he just stalling, getting up his nerve to tell his story?

"Well, boys, I ain't one to be afraid of a danged long haired woman. Never saw one I figured to be worth the time of day, anyhow. But that damned ghost we saw last night must have been meaner than hell when she was alive. She's got no respect fer nothing or nobody." Rube had everybody's attention and wanted the telling to last a while.

"What'd she do, Rube? How'd she look? How long did she let you stay? Don't keep us in suspense," said Jake. Rube glared at him, not wanting to be hurried.

"Well, the rest of you know how Jake and Doc left us there at that infested cabin without our horses?" He watched the heads nod.

"Yeah, we heard that much," said a neighbor. "We thought you uz crazy."

"Me and Jim first went for a walk down to the creek, jest to look around and to get some water fer coffee. It was a real pretty evening with the sun painting the clouds all sorts of colors. They wuz a little breeze blowing and we set out under the pecan tree fer a spell. Then we decided to go in when it began getting dark. We picked up a little kindling and some sticks fer a fire from that old woodpile as we went in. Jim made the coffee after I got a little fire going in the fireplace. Somebody left an oil lamp in there, so we had a little light. It started out to be a right peaceful evening."

Jim, with a scowl on his face, stood to the side listening to his brother. He knew better than to try to hurry Rube. Being the younger of the two he had learned patience back when he was also the smaller of the two, but he hated to admit the fear they had shared the night before. He grunted loud enough for Jim to hear and know he wanted the story over with.

"Well, about midnight we unrolled our bedrolls on top of that old bed frame. There's not much room in that cabin, you know, and then we got all settled to go to sleep. Just as we dozed off we heard a sort of a shriek and both set up in bed real sudden-like. 'What's that?' I asked Jim."

"Damned if I know, he said. We'd left the lamp lit because if someone tried to scare us we wanted to be able to see to shoot," said Rube. No one doubted they would have been shot. The Burr boys had the reputation of being crack shots with short fuses.

"About that time that danged woman, if you could call her that, came right through the log wall! She didn't come through the door or window, nor down the chimney. She jest came right through the wall!" Rube looked around to make sure everyone understood.

"What'd she look like?" asked Jake.

"Like nothing I ever seen or hope to see! Man, she was horrible ugly—with a skull face that had skin dried and hanging in places, matted ugly hair…and the stink! She sorta danced around and on the table, all the time making weird noises and shaking long bony fingers at us. But it was the feeling of hate that got me the most. Weren't no mistaking what she felt about US. It was pure hate. It was like she enjoyed scaring, and like she was getting ready to enjoy tearing us apart. She went through the roof once, and we thought she was gone, but she come right back. She finally got more toward the fireplace, away from between us and the door, and we decided not to stay for the encore. We grabbed our pants and boots and ran."

Rube and Jim Burr didn't stay in Erath County long after their encounter with Jenny, not because of it, but because their secret was found out. That Sunday morning the report reached

Alexander that the Texas and Pacific train had been robbed east of Benbrook for the last two Friday nights in a row. The Fort Worth sheriff had found a slicker near the robbery site with a label that showed it had been bought at Bishop and Gillete Mercantile, a store in Alexander. So he was down asking questions. Ben Green told him about Jim Burr using his filly those two nights and the big fee he paid for her use.

The sheriff rode to the door of Rube's and Jim's house, but Jim, the big one, came to the door with a Winchester in his hand and a mean glint in his eyes. The sheriff, not wanting to commit suicide, just passed the time of day and headed back to town for help. The Burrs didn't wait for a showdown, they just rode off. As it turned out, there were five men in on the robberies, and those two train hold-ups were just links in a chain of robberies over about two years' time. They had robbed trains in Alabama before coming to Texas, and went from Texas to Oklahoma for more. Wells Fargo was offering a reward. Once, when they were cornered after pulling a job in Oklahoma, they shot several officers. They were infamous enough to outshine the James Boys in the eyes of those who were knowledgeable about daring and law-breaking. Finally the rewards got big enough that they met their doom when local people identified them, but several books were written telling about their daring escapades.

After hearing the Burrs' tale of the ghost, Dr. Jed was even more determined than ever to try to communicate with Jenny. Holding in his mind the vision he had beheld for just a few seconds of a beautiful red-haired woman with the sorrowful expression coming toward him, he clung to the belief that they shared some common bond. Never mind the gruesome apparition that had made believers of many people, braver people than Doc. As far as he knew, he and Sam were the only ones who had seen the other Jenny. Maybe she knew he meant her no harm. She must sense something in him that was different. Certainly his troubled soul yearned for understanding .

He didn't know how he was different, or even how others perceived him, but Jed knew he had walked through "the valley of the shadow of death" and was a better man for having done so. In his first years of medical practice he had the knowledge and the skill, but he could only put patches on bodies and encourage healing of the physical person. His manner was aloof, and try as he might to be cordial, polite, he remained an outsider. It seemed that when he was called to treat an accidental injury, he had to bite his tongue to keep from saying things like, "Well, you should have known better than to try that stupid thing," —whatever it was that caused the accident—or "Well, if you hadn't been drinking you could have avoided that injury." He was a rational man, always able to attribute causes to illnesses and hurts; causes brought on by human ignorance, or greed, or foolhardiness, or pride. Using the modicum of brain power that God gave man to separate him from the beasts, made most accidents and many ills avoidable. So, Jed slapped on the patches but still hated himself for being unable to help all those hungry, hurting spirits.

Having loving, understanding, Christian parents with money enough to meet their needs and most of Jed's wants had made his childhood and adolescent days comfortable. Until much later, he experienced no great hardships, no death of loved ones, no life-threatening trauma. His knowledge about such pain had not matured into wisdom and empathy, and so he remained an outsider living on the decorative fringe of suffering humanity. And then tragedy came.

Sitting under the pecan tree that evening late, Dr. Jed, known simply as Doc to his friends and patients as a sign of their acceptance, a testimony to the change in his personality, recalled those hours of suffering when he had sat by Florence's bedside, holding her hand, watching her gain consciousness and then lose it again. Holding his anger at bay as he willed her to fight for life, as he felt her pain, humiliation and loss of faith in people, he began to understand the foolishness and cruelty of man against himself and others. Only his love, shown by his nearness and loving expressions of tenderness, not his expertise in nursing and doctoring, had helped Florence make the choice to live when dying would have been so much easier and less painful. For the first time in his life he was able to put himself in another's place, to feel vicarious pain and anguish. He began to understand now the sense of violation, of outrage that Florence felt. He felt the damage to her psyche, and his own suffered deep wounds, too deep to know how they could be expressed.

Nursing her back to health gave him much opportunity for soul searching and to develop a determination to grow more sensitive to others. But at the same time, destructive forces of hate and desire for revenge fed upon his doubt.

Although he tried to curb those demands while he concentrated on helping Florence, she was sensitive and knew his feelings. Soon, she was the nurturing one, trying to lessen his feelings of hatred. Together they wrestled with all the terrible aftermath of the attack, and in their search for peace, they grew closer until they were one. The move to Erath and a life with fewer outside demands had helped.

Jed drank in the beauty of the sunset and wished Florence were there to share it. Had she been with him on both occasions, she would have known that the squirrel sharing his shade today was the same one that risked his presence on the other occasion, because Florence had a knack for detecting the individual characteristics of animals, her hens, and, most of all, people.

"Looks like Jenny might not honor us with her presence today," he said to the squirrel.

Jenny was there. She was gloating because she had become so skilled in grotesqueness. The power she had found in terrifying people who invaded her space was a heady experience. Being a wandering spirit had its advantages. Instead of living in fear as she had those months in the cabin, especially when Charlie was gone, she was now in control and enjoyed seeing fear in others, especially men like those cocky bastards who were there last night. They had come with all their male righteousness and conceit.

"Ain't no woman gonna run me off," she remembered hearing the little one say. "Dumb broads! Just good fer one thing alive, and that makes a damn ghost good fer nothing."

She was enjoying the triumph of those minutes when Rube and Jim fought each other to get through the door first, when absolute terror was the controlling force in their lives. Ahh, sweet revenge! Her ghostly gloating was interrupted when Jed came. At first, she gathered her energy, selected her image, and prepared to make an entrance. Then she sensed a difference in Doc. She felt no conceit, no pretensions, no lording it over others, and she hesitated in the effort to understand. Quieting her powers, she began to sense a little of what the man was thinking, and it was a completely new experience. She sat, invisible, in wonder, at the edge of the shade and watched until the sun went down.

The squirrel had run up the tree, but Doc talked to him just the same.

"Tis a peaceful place, in spite of what others say. I feel like Jenny knows I'm here. Hope she knows a little of what I feel. I'm really a peaceful fool. Guess I'll go along now. The hens will have gone to roost without their corn. I'll have to get up early in the morning and make it up to them. Good night, friend." Jed didn't know whether he was talking to the squirrel or to Jenny, but he was sure something heard him.

CHAPTER X

Soon-Lou

"Doc, Sam Keith says for you to ride over soon as you come in. Sally's worse," Jake was delivering a message to Doc at noon.

"Guess I'd better not eat then, Jake. Sam wouldn't have sent for me unless it was urgent. Sally's been down with pneumonia for four or five days now. Can't seem to get any better." Doc was worried. He made a mental check of the medications he had in his bag and knew that none of them was really going to make a whole lot of difference. "Give me some coffee Jake, and have Miguel to roll me something in a tortilla to eat on the way."

"Is she real bad, Doc?" asked Jake.

"I'm afraid she is. I'm about ready for any help I can get. Seems like a strong woman like Sally would respond to something, but she's not getting any better."

"Maybe I oughtn't to say this, but have you thought of getting old Soon-Lou over there? She came once when my sister-in-law was sick and gave her some Indian cure. It helped her. It weren't pneumonia she had, but she was real sick. That was before you came to Alexander," said Jake.

"I've heard of her, Jake, and was thinking of asking her if she could help. No doubt about it, those Indian doctors know how to cure lots of things," said Doc. "We may not hold much with their spirit chants and dancing around, but they know about herbs and natural healing. I've seen it happen."

"Well, I reckon she'd be willing. She seems like a good woman," said Jake .

"Why is she content to stay at Sikes with her daughter, anyway? Looks like she would want to go with her own people."

"Soon-Lou keeps to herself mostly, but she's got a crippled leg after a bad break one time. Someone said she wasn't able to make the long march to the reservation in Oklahoma when they took the Caddos up there. Don't never see her around 'cept when she comes in with George Sikes to get some of her medicine supplies that she can't find in the woods, stuff like cinnamon. Don't know how they got things like that before the white man came. Maybe they traded more than we imagine," Jake said.

"Or they may have learned to make medicines using cinnamon after the settlers came. Never know. Tell you what, Jake. Is there someone here that could go tell Soon-Lou to come to the Keiths'?"

"Sure thing, Doc. I'll find someone. Soon-Lou may be there by the time you are."

Chester Brownlow, with a foot on the bar rail and cradling a whiskey in his big hand was listening to the conversation. "You ain't gonna let some dirty squaw near Sally are you? No telling what she'll do. She may give her poison." Chester was a little soaked, but he wouldn't have been any more agreeable had he been completely sober.

"Well, now, Chester. I'm sorry to hear you say that," said Doc. He had neither the time nor the desire to argue with Chester today.

You'll be sorrier yet if you listen to that no good Indian. I'd never have her in my house, you can bet on that. Can't never trust those dogs."

"Chester, it's a good thing it's not your wife that's sick," said Jake.

"Yeah, my wife knows better than to get sick."

Doc didn't stay to hear more. He took the food Miguel handed him and left.

Sam Keith had been on his farm long enough to make some additions to his original log cabin. The old part, floored after the first two years, now served as a big comfortable kitchen with a fireplace and also a wood cookstove. He had added a dog-trot and two more rooms, a bed room and one that served as a bed-sitting room stretched east of the kitchen.

Sam had moved a bed into the kitchen for Sally since she had been sick. It was the only room in the house that really stayed warm, and he could better care for her and tend to chores at the same time. Nights in October were pretty cool, and Sally kept kicking the covers off. She wavered between consciousness and unconsciousness as she struggled to keep breathing. When Doc walked in he was struck by the strangeness of seeing the strong active Sally looking so pale and weak, and by the familiar smell of sickness that met him. Sally's straw-colored hair, usually slicked back in a knot on the back of her head was tousled and as dry looking as a tumbleweed. Her prominent forehead made her eyes look sunken and wild. She took no notice of Doc as he traded places with Sam who had been sponging her face and arms with cold water. He took her pulse and temperature, and was trying to decide what more to do when the dog in the yard began to bark.

George Sikes and Soon-Lou rode up to the door. The old Caddo woman, ancient beyond her years, said not a word as she sniffed the air of the sickroom, knelt by the bed, took Sally's hand, and laid her ear to the chest of the sick woman. She then went to the stove where water was boiling in the iron kettle, and took from her belt a leather bag.

Doc asked no questions as he watched. Sam was helping George take care of the horses. With solemn seriousness Soon-Lou selected a crock cream pitcher and began mixing herbs. Doc recognized the odor of cinnamon and cloves as the heavy fragrance rose when she poured the boiling water into the pitcher. He guessed at the hemlock bark, but of other ingredients he had no clue. As he was wondering if it would be offensive to ask, he jumped back in shock! Without warning Soon-lou began a shrill chant. She stood with her face up, showing her prominent bony nose and chin in profile. A long gray braid fell down her back to below the waist as she sang with very little movement of her lips, her eyes shut and her hands lifted in supplication. At first, she was as still as death, and then she began to sway with the song which became a keening wail echoing about the room. It even scared Sam at the stables.

"Don't be affeared, Sam. That's jest Soon-Lou's way of praying. I reckon she prays to the same God we do, but she sure does it different. I've got used to it some. She's a wise woman, I've decided," said George. The pride in his voice did more to allay Sam's fear than did the words.

Back in the sick room, Doc watched as the Indian began to bow. Then, abruptly she stopped, opened her eyes, and checked the contents of the pitcher. She poured some into a cup, went to the bed and lifted Sally's head. Muttering and coaxing, she managed to get the sick woman to drink a few swallows. She sat very still and watched until in just a few minutes Sally began to sweat profusely. Soon-Lou mopped Sally's face and repeated the procedure about fifteen minutes later. Doc waited around to watch for awhile, then, satisfied with what he saw, and finding that he could be of no help, he went to the barn to visit with Sam and George.

"How's she doing, Doc?" Sam asked anxiously.

"Well, Sam, last time Soon-Lou put that cup of medicine to her lips, she swallowed without much coaxing. I'd say she's just a tad better."

"That's good. Soon-Lou knows how to handle sickness. I ain't saying she's better than you, Doc. Reckon there's room fer both of you round here," George said.

"If she can help Sally, I'm just glad we got her," said Doc.

"Reckon she trusts you too, Doc. Remember she had us call you when we lost that baby. And when my son Albert broke his leg she gave him something to ease the pain but insisted I go for you to set the bone. Another time he had the trots real bad, though, she mixed up some of them herbs and treated him herself," George said.

"Sure hope her herbs is what Sally needs. It's real scary when she gets sick enough to go to bed. In fact, jest one other time, except when the children was born, did she ever give up and go to bed." Sam thought of several times when he had had the flu and she nursed him day and night.

"Soon-Lou's got some strange ways, but they seem to work. She's a plumb good gardener. She and Ruth Ann have a vegetable garden by the house and she grows lots of stuff. Has it earlier than anyone in the county, I'll bet. But I don't know where she got some of her ideas. Last spring I looked out the door early one morning and there she was with a straw broom beating the tomato vines. I swore a little and was going to rush out to stop her, but Ruth Ann grabbed my arm and explained. The tomato vines kept growing bigger and bigger, but they weren't blooming. Ruth Ann said Soon-Lou was beating the plants so they would bloom. Well-sir, I didn't go stop her, but I didn't believe them tomatoes knew what they was getting a beating fer. But you know, in just a few days they was blooming like a blackberry vine, jest all over blossoms. We had more tomatoes than we could ever eat."

"Well I'll be derned. Never heard of the likes. But it musta worked. I remember you brought us some of them fine tomatoes," Sam said and scratched his head.

"Guess we could all learn some things from the Indians. I want to talk to her about some of her remedies. I've heard that they pick just one or two selected children each generation to teach the old ways of doctoring," said Doc.

"I tell you for a fact, I've learned some things from her," said her son-in-law. "One lesson is not to laugh at the old ways. But, you know, when we was coming over here she had to stop at the ghost hole and do some weird things. She always does. Never mind we're in a hurry, or what. And she never will let me stay with her, says I don't make harmony with the spirits. So she sends me on up the road a piece. But this evening I stayed close enough to watch her, wanted to hurry her up a bit. But here's what she done. First she took a cup outen her sack and went down to the water and got a cup full. She took it back to the pecan tree, went around under the limb where Charlie and them other men were strung up and sprinkled the ground with the water. Then she stood on the other side of the tree and made her arms like she was holding a baby and she rocked and crooned a bit. Next, she turned her head back and sung one of them chants of hers. Didn't take long till she come on up the trail and got back on her horse."

Doc was very interested in the story. "Tell me about the hanging, Sam. I heard a little about it, but don't know any particulars."

"Well that was a strange thing. Musta been a morning about like this one, though now that I think on it, it was in September. Like to scared the wits out of me when Charlie come stumbling in the house with Temple crying and trying to help him. His neck was swollen and blue as a mulberry. Took him awhile to tell me what happened, but he finally did." Sam told Doc the story of the hanging, how Temple cut his pa down and saved him.

"Charlie decided they should head for Oklahoma Territory the next morning. I had to agree with him. They ain't no way you can fight those vigilante devils because you never know who they are, or who they'll have it in for next. So I loaned Charlie a horse, the vigilantes took his, said they was stolen property. We agreed for me to finish up his crop to pay for the horse, but I got a letter from him about the next year with money in it to pay for the horse. Would've sent it back, but he didn't give no address. Told me to take whatever else of his stuff I wanted. He couldn't stand to think of coming back to get any of it."

"What about revenge, Sam? Seems to me he'd be eaten up with the desire to get back at whoever killed his wife. Maybe not for his hanging so much as for Jenny's murder," said Doc, recognizing his own feelings.

"Well, he was at first. He kept prowling and asking around. If you ask me, that's why the vigilantes came fer him. What do you think, George?" asked Sam.

"I think you're right, Sam. I know he had someone sweating, but he wouldn't tell me who he suspected. Look, Soon-Lou's waving from the porch."

Sam took off running for the house. George and Doc went more slowly. When they got there they heard Sally.

"Oh Sam. I'm sorry." She was too weak to say more.

"Nothing to be sorry fer, Sal. You jest sleep, now." Without embarrassment he wiped his tears on the back of his hand and as gently as he could rubbed her hair back and held her hand as she sighed and slept.

Soon-Lou stayed that night and the next day to continue nursing and doctoring, but Sally was soon up and gaining strength.

"The moon came up, and the path was a ribbon of
silver in front of me. There's something silent about
moonlight. It's not light It's a state of things When
there was sound it was unexpected, like the sudden
shiver on the flank of a sleeping beast "
—Geoffrey Household
Taboo

CHAPTER XI

Woman in the Moonlight

George and Doctor Jed Eakins rode along together after
seeing that Soon-Lou had everything she needed to care
for Sally, and that Sally was on the mend.

"How does it make you feel, Doc, when an old Indian cures
one of your patients?" asked George.

"Well, I guess when you're at the end of your rope, you
appreciate a helping hand whatever direction it comes from.
But to tell the truth, I have a lot of respect for Indian medicine
and know-how. Long before white men came to these parts,
the Inde, as the Apaches call "the people," were living in
harmony with the land and animals. My guess is they studied
the animals to see what plants were edible and which ones to
avoid. Animals seem to know what to eat, and when—if it's
available to them. But the Inde have passed that knowledge on
to their people for centuries."

"Yeah, I suppose. My wife has some peculiar ways, she and
her mama. But they are kind and gentle. Ruth Ann says her
mama named her 'Peace Maker,' or a name that meant that. She

was called Ruth Ann by the teachers on the reservation. But she's lived up to her name," said George.

"Women have a wonderful gentling influence on men, don't they, George?"

"Yep, you're right about that. It'd be a mighty rough and dirty place without them," George agreed.

"But not all women, and not all the time for any particular woman. Guess they come in all kinds. I remember the preacher a while back talking about it's better to live on a house top than with a contentious woman. Sure would be hard to live on house tops like we got here—but guess it sure would be hard to live with a contrary woman," mused Doc.

They were getting near the McDow, just at sundown. The colors in the sky were soft and brilliant at the same time, like they can be on a hot humid day in Texas. Silence hung heavy, except for the lonesome call of a whip-poor-will in a willow on the creek bank, and it seemed so much a part of the mood of the place that it was felt rather than heard. Only the smell of smoke from a wood fire which had drifted to the hollow of the creek hinted of human promise. The sound of their horses as they walked along seemed loud, and the comforting cloak of their own voices encouraged conversation.

"Reckon Jenny was a contentious woman?" asked George.

"She just might have been, from what I've heard about her. I don't think she started fights, or nagged at Charlie, but her discontent must have charged the atmosphere," said Doc.

"What do you mean, charged the atmosphere?" asked George.

"Well, you know how an evening can feel when there's a storm brewing. Like tonight. When it's still, the air seems heavy, and thunderclouds are building in the southwest. It's like you expect the lightning to split the sky at any minute, but you don't see any, yet. It just seems to keep you watching." Doc said.

"I guess I know what you mean. My women folks always read the weather. They seem in tune to all them signs," said George.

"I think Jenny kept the air tense with feelings like that. She didn't exactly stir things up, but I guess Charlie always felt like he couldn't quite live up to her expectations. I think she stored up anger and resentment against him. You know, let little irritations grow like green mold. It must have caused him heartache to realize she didn't feel at home here. And even now, she has to stay."

George was silent, still puzzling over Doc's sayings, getting the feel but not sure of the words. They had come to the water hole and were letting their horses drink.

Suddenly George's horse lifted her head, then ducked it and gave a mighty kick! George grabbed the saddlehorn and yelled, "Whoa, Moche! Whoa, now! What in tarnation's wrong with you!"

Doc's horse followed suit. Both splashed through the water and up the east bank, nearly leaving the riders in the water, but they held on for dear life! Doc looked back and there was Jenny waving her arms threateningly.

"Look, George! She's there. Jenny's behind us!"

George looked back and then spurred his horse even harder. He took the trail to the north without another word, and Doc turned toward Alexander.

Doc had just gotten to the Papworth barn when he decided to control his fright and stop. Rather than try to gentle his horse and coax her to go back, he led her a short way down the lane and tied her to the rail fence in front of the cabin. Then he slowly walked back toward the pecan tree. Feeling his heart pounding in his neck, he felt both his fear and his determination to overcome it. He wondered about his motives for being in that situation as he stopped and looked at the lingering colors in the western sky. Taking a few deep breaths, he looked up at the stars that seemed almost close enough to touch.

"Real restful sky," he said to himself and whoever else might be listening. "Wonder why anybody—or any spirit—would take offense on a night like this?"

He mentally searched his consciousness to determine if he had reason to rush home, but his sense of urgency subsided as he could think of no real reason to do so. Deciding to follow his curious intuitive feelings, instead of the impulse to flee, he looked all around him in the twilight.

"Chickens have already gone to roost anyway, and with that harvest moon coming up I'll have no trouble seeing the lane. Can't say I'd really prefer to keep company with a ghost after dark, but I don't think Jenny really has reason to want to harm me." He sat with his back to the tree, facing east this time to watch the moon rise.

"Don't think anyone else will be coming. I'd hate for them to hear me talking to myself out here. They might send me off to a lockup somewhere, and here I am planning to go to a medical convention in New Orleans next month." He thought about that for a few minutes. Time he got in contact with colleagues. Maybe some big advances had been made. His experience with Soon-Lou made him more than ever aware of his limitations. But his mind was made up about that trip. No use dwelling on details. He'd go.

"You know, Jenny, I think I can understand some of your feelings. A bunch of them used to rule my life, too. Don't know how Florence ever put up with me, but I sure needed her gentling. Some folks are just naturally good, I suppose. Hard for me to understand freely given unselfishness and forgiveness in big measure.

"Now I wonder about that time when the vigilantes came for Charlie. You've been scaring everyone else from off this place. How come you couldn't help him? Didn't you want to?" As he thought about that for a few minutes, he seemed to know the answer. "Takes time to learn about being a spirit. Guess you can't jump right into all the powers and ways of life outside the body. Come to think about it, that happened before anyone had reported seeing you, if I've got the stories sorted out right. But you could see them, couldn't you? How helpless you must have felt when those bastards rode up and you saw right through their hoods to the mean, weak men hidden underneath, you must have been fearfully aware of the danger to Charlie and Temple. Did you keep the boy hidden down on the creek so he would be safe until they were gone? Was it your coaching that made that young boy know what to do to save his pa? Maybe you lifted up on the rope to help save his life. No, I don't suppose you could physically interfere. It was just lucky that Charlie was on the end."

Doc pictured the scene in his mind. He could feel the danger as the vigilantes rode up, and he sensed outrage and hatred. Was it from Jenny? Did she know and have reason to hate one or more of the men in the hanging party? Yes, he thought she did. As he sat there in the moonlight, aware of a ghostly presence, he understood her hatred when she recognized the man who killed her baby in the lynching mob.

"Funny thing about hate, Jenny, it's like a festering boil. I've doctored many a boil. Seen them rise up, get red all around, hurt like hell, especially if they receive a blow right on the head.

Then, they get ripe and you can begin to help them heal. Some soaking and draining and lots of cleansing. Soon they get well. Hate's like that. It festers and hurts and spreads all around. Left on its own, with no cleansing and protection, it can make a person sick to death. Resentment builds up and saps all the good thoughts and feelings a person is likely to have." He thought of that first year after Florence had been attacked and how revenge and planning for revenge took all his thoughts. Just when Florence needed tenderness and reassurances of love and worth, he was eaten up with anger and hate. "Seems to strangle all the good impulses a fellow might have.

"It takes forgiveness, Jenny. Forgiveness of others—without their even asking or knowing. But I guess the hardest thing is to forgive yourself. Most important, too, but the hardest for me to do. I couldn't go back and right the wrong, and had to forgive myself for all those things that might have prevented the attack—better locks, being home, warning Florence to be careful—nothing but humanness to forgive myself for. But I made a hell out of it.

"It takes forgiveness. When we moved out here, away from the scene, when I saw human goodness in action, I began to understand what Florence had gone through, the natural progressions she let God work in her, but that I would have no part of. Finally, it's happened to me—almost against my own will power, but I'm getting there. Maybe you will, too, some day. Guess you could still do it after you're a ghost. Perhaps it's never too late for that kind of comfort."

Doc thought of Soon-Lou and her willingness to help Sally. How she must have had to lay aside all the grievances her people held against the white man to be able to intercede for one of them.

"Of course, no one could want anything but good for Sally. She's been a mainstay around here always. But Soon-Lou and her people have reason to be full of hate and resentment toward all white folks. You know who I'm talking about. I understand she recognizes you every time she comes this way. We could both learn much from her, couldn't we? Well, now, the moon is getting on up there, guess it's time for me to go."

In spite of his confidence that Jenny would be friendly to him, the hair on the back of his neck rose and goose bumps prickled as he saw a woman walk between him and the lane where his horse was tied. She seemed to float more than walk in the moonlight. Her white dress fluttered behind her as if blown by a wind he couldn't feel. He turned to watch as the breeze seemed to carry her on toward the creek. He edged toward his horse. As he reached for the rein, he paused with his hand lifted as he heard a soft moan catch in a throat with a sob. The ghost lifted a hand and waved to him.

CHAPTER XII

Franklin and Millie

After throwing the last pitchfork of hay to the mule he had been plowing with all day, Franklin took off his stained hat and wiped the sweat from his brow. It had been a hard hot day, and after finishing the field nearest the house, he was glad to quit a little early. As he stretched his long arms over his head, feeling the welcome cool where the breeze blew through the sweat-wet blue duck, he wrinkled his nose at the rancid smell and headed for the water trough.

"Poor cows. Guess they won't mind a little honest sweat in their water," he said as he took off his shirt and splashed water on his lean body.

Millie's father had come by from his farm near Dublin early that morning. He was on his way to Stephenville to trade for two horses and would be back to the Gilstraps' to stay that night. Millie wanted Franklin to finish chores in time for an early supper so they could visit a little.

Although in her thirties and the mother of two sons, Millie was still the favorite daughter of Hiram Clark. Hiram didn't mind telling Franklin every time they visited, "You not only got my smartest daughter, Franklin, you also got my only son."

It wasn't beauty that made Millie a favorite of her father's, nor was it some delicate charm that had won Franklin's heart. With a big, rather hooked nose—only a little smaller than her father's—and little, deep-set, light brown eyes, she was homely, until her joy and celebration of living had occasion to show. Her big hands and feet proclaimed her sturdiness. Having given up ever fathering a son when Millie, the third of four daughters was born, Hiram had treated her like a boy. She was the one who worked with her father, hunted with her father, and even competed with him in sharp shooting and riding. They hunted deer in the fall and bobcat, timber wolves, or any other predators when the need arose. So, any time Hiram had occasion to be in the neighborhood, going to the county seat, to the depot, or just to buy supplies, he stopped by Franklin and Millie's to see his grandsons, but especially to see their mother. Franklin was always glad to see him.

The Gilstrap house consisted of one large room with a half loft where the boys, aged six and eight, slept. Franklin and Millie were gradually adding improvements. They had a windmill with a large wooden tank elevated to add pressure so that soon they hoped to have water piped to the house. Given the choice of such a luxury or another room added to their cabin, they had chosen the water.

Millie hadn't neglected to develop her domestic talents when she grew up as a tomboy. She could cook and sew and used ingenuity to make their home comfortable. She had used flour sacks, dyed deep blue, to make a curtain to give a little privacy to one corner of the house for a bedroom. Another bed, a narrow cot, served as a seat when it wasn't needed as a bed.

The cabin had two doors, front and back, and three windows. Since most of the cold wind came from the north, that side of the house had been left without either door or window. The front door opened from the left, and on the wall to the left was not one but two gun racks. Franklin kept his gun on one and Millie had hers on the other. Hiram had arrived about sundown, and placed his gun on the floor under the rack.

It was cozy in the cabin, although a little warm, where the family finished eating venison stew and cornbread for supper by the light of the oil lamp. The heat from the wood stove and the aroma of the stew rich with onions and potatoes blended with the smell of burning cedar to give those who could smell it a feeling of peace and well-being. In late October darkness came early hugging the family together in the glow of the lamp. Interrupting their visiting, catching up on news of family connections and goings-on, they heard horses approaching. Since the vigilantes had made everyone so nervous, the Gilstraps didn't take unnecessary chances.

"Hit the loft, boys. Get up there and stay put till I find out who our visitors are," said Franklin as he set the lamp on a little table which would be sheltered from the wind when the door was opened. Wouldn't take much to blow the light out. The Gilstrap boys were trained to obey without question, a necessary way of life in frontier country. Millie and Hiram remained seated at the table, not visible to the approaching riders since the light was moved.

Franklin automatically reached for his gun as he opened the door to a scene that made him tremble with apprehension. The flicker of six torches dancing in the south wind added a ghost-like glow to the sight of ten hooded riders! Franklin held his gun in his right hand with the barrel cradled in the bend of his left arm. With his feet firmly planted, his back straight and stiff, his voice showed determination as he faced the gruesome mob.

"State your business," he said.

A man at the front of the group with a piece of rope in his hand dismounted and said, "Mr. Gilstrap, you are looking at justice. Three strange horses were seen in your barn lot this evening about sundown. We know that you are part of a ring of horse thieves that brought those horses from Granbury. No doubt someone will be here tomorrow to pick them up and drive them on to western markets. We've come to see that you pay for your crimes."

"You're not hanging me!" Franklin shouted and fired his gun into the air, bringing it around to aim at the man with the rope when a shot came from the rider on a paint horse just behind the hooded one on foot and knocked the gun from Franklin's hand.

About that time two other figures stepped to the door and another shot rang out. Millie, true to aim, had shot the vigilante on the paint horse. He fell to the ground.

As two others were about to dismount to rescue their leader, Hiram commanded, "Leave him be! Ride out of here or more will fall!" Then he and Millie, with guns at the ready, stepped outside the door.

"Get on your horse, you murderer," said Franklin, reaching for the hood of the man on foot. "If I find out who you are, I'll hunt you down and show you some justice."

The nine hooded horsemen turned and fled. Franklin and Hiram picked up the fallen vigilante, carried him into the cabin and laid him on the cot. He was still breathing, but bleeding profusely from a chest wound. They removed the hood to reveal the face of Chester Brownlow!

After discussing the situation, the three adults decided that for any one of them to go out alone that night to get the doctor was too dangerous. The vigilantes had to protect their identity, and might be hiding to waylay a lone rider. If they stayed there together, having advertised their arms and expertise with them, they were probably in little danger. Early in the morning Mr. Clark would go for the doctor. In the meantime, they managed to stop the bleeding and make the unconscious Brownlow as comfortable as possible.

Hiram left before daylight to ride a circuitous route into Alexander. He first went by Sam and Sally Keith's house and told them of the shooting. Sam rode back with him to the Gilstraps' and Sally rode to tell Katherine that Chester had been shot, and to stay with the baby and little boy while Katherine went to be with her husband.

Katherine and Doc got to the bedside about the same time. She went in quietly, looked at her husband and sat silently with bowed head.

Doc took Chester's pulse, listened to his breathing, pulled the packing away to inspect the wound and quietly replaced it. "Looks like you did all anyone could do, Millie. He's too weak to do any probing for the bullet. He's bled internally a great deal."

"Will he live, Doc?" asked Millie in a quietly anxious voice.

"We'll just have to wait and see. If he rallies in the next hour we may be able to help him. But I really don't expect him to. Sounds like his lungs are filling with fluid."

Millie put her hand on Katherine's shoulder. "I'm so sorry, Kathie, I'm so sorry I shot Chester."

"It couldn't be helped. I tried to tell him that sooner or later someone was going to kill him. He never did listen to me."

Katherine spoke mechanically, without emotion. All the feeling she had for her husband had long since been spent.

Suddenly, wild and glassy eyed, Chester Brownlow tried to sit up. "Get her out of here! Don't let her come near me!" His terror-filled eyes riveted on something or someone invisible to the others in the room.

"Take it easy, Brownlow. No one is going to hurt you!" said Doc.

"Get her out of here! Get that woman out of here!"

"Who do you see?" asked Doc.

"It's her! It's Jenny Papworth! That woman has been after me for years," said Chester.

"But Chester, Jenny's dead," said Millie.

CHAPTER XIII

The Séance

It was a combination going-away party for Doc Eakins and a regular "dinner on the ground" for the church. Last month they had met to say goodbye to Mrs. Brownlow and make preparations to help her and her kids get things ready to take the train back to her folks in Tennessee. Brownlow had been dead about six months, and the community had rallied together to help his family through hard times. Now, everyone wondered if the ghost of Jenny was still around, or if, perhaps, she had found rest.

"Well, Doc, it's nice of you to warn us we can't be sick for the next month, but are you sure it will be all right to get the croup six weeks from now?" asked Sam.

"Can't say it would be advisable—unless that New Orleans meeting has more knowledge than I imagine it has. Not much to do for croup except wear it out. But if you're asking if I'll be back, the answer is yes." Dr. Jed stopped talking to try his coffee, but one sip showed it was still too hot to drink. The rich aroma brought a sigh of contentment—or was it the peace of the occasion? His friends and neighbors waited patiently. No use hurrying good conversation. "I considered just going on somewhere else. Don't really have much here to come back to," said Doc.

"You got friends here, Doc. What's the rest of the world got fer you?" asked Franklin.

"You've got me there, Franklin. I have no hankering to go back to city life. Why, patients there expect you to wear one of those white starched jackets. My old horse would throw me for sure if I came out in one of those. At least, I feel sort of a part of this community."

"I used to think we had more comers than goers around here. But seems like we've had more leavers lately," said Sam. "Of course, some just get discouraged or seek greener pastures, but seems like we have our share of runners, too."

"Speaking of runners, wonder whatever happened to Charlie Papworth? I get the feeling he wasn't very interested in finding out who killed Jenny. Wonder if he knows Brownlow confessed?" asked Doc.

"Ain't got no idea, but I reckon you ain't reading facts right about him being a runner. Truth of the matter's he had no choice a'tall, as I see it. He was a troubled man, full of doubt and guilt. When he was with us he was always asking, 'Why did I leave her? Why did I try to keep her here when she was so unhappy?' and things like that all the time." Sam took another bite of the chocolate cake he was eating and brushed crumbs off his ample stomach. "He tried to find out who killed her and, no doubt, would have killed the guilty man, but once the vigilantes got on to him, and he survived that hanging, he had to leave. They would have got him next time for sure, because they were afraid he'd recognized someone."

"I suppose you're right. Just seems a shame," agreed Doc.

"After that hanging, when he came to get a horse, he said that the only thing that mattered to him now was the boy, Temple, and he was going to take him away from this place with such memories. May not have helped—but Charlie was a good man," said Sam.

"Speaking of Papworths, has anyone seen Jenny lately?"

"Did you hear about them spiritualists that came looking for her?" asked Sam.

"Spiritualists? When was that?" asked Doc.

"Why, just the other day. They said they wanted to act as a 'rescue circle.' They claimed that some folks are dead, but don't really know they're dead. Then the spirit wanders around kinda lost and lonesome. One of them 'rescue circles' is supposed to teach the spirit its business, " said Sam.

"Tarnation! I never heard the likes of that! Imagine trying to teach a lost spirit. How in thunder would you go about that?" asked Franklin.

"It do sound foolish, I grant. They claimed you had to have a thing they called a say-ance, I think that's what they call it," said Sam.

"I think it's called a 'seance,'" Doc said. "I've heard of them. These folks get together in a dimly lit room and try to call up a few spirits."

"Yeah, that's it. A seance. Sally can tell you more about it than I can. They talked her into helping them. Hey, Sal, all these folks would like to hear about your experience with the Stevensons. Why don't you tell them about it."

The ladies were sitting on one of the church benches brought out under the trees. Dinner was over and visiting was in full swing. The men edged a little closer to the women so that everyone could hear.

Sally, in a pretty blue dress that matched her eyes and softened the angles of her face, didn't mind being the center of attention. She knew she could tell a story as well as anyone, and enjoyed doing it.

"Well, there was a Mr. and Mrs. Stevenson and Mrs. Stevenson's sister Ruby. Don't remember her last name. They called her Ruby. They came driving up in their buggy…Monday it was, 'cause I was building a fire under the wash pot. I invited them up on the porch to see what their business was.

"'Mrs. Keith,' said this Mr. Stevenson, 'we've heard about a troubled spirit in your neighborhood, and we came to help her.'

"Well, you can guess I was flabbergasted. Not that I wouldn't want to help Jenny, but whoever heard of helping a ghost? Still, I was willing to listen. They explained about their 'rescue circle' and how they could contact spirits. I didn't have much faith in their plans. Sounded like a bunch of foolishness to me—but they seemed harmless. They wanted me to be a part of their circle. Said they needed someone that had known Jenny. Someone that Jenny would trust. I kept tellin' them that I didn't know anything about contacting spirits. Truth is, I wasn't really keen on the idea of being able to call up a haint, but they insisted that I didn't need to know anything about it. All I needed to do was sit in a circle with them, holding hands, and they'd do whatever else was necessary.

"Anyway, Sam was right about me having a bushel of curiosity. I wanted to know if Jenny was still around and if they could talk to her. So I agreed to take them to the cabin and sit with them—didn't really think Sam would mind wearing dirty clothes one more day. I got in the back of the buggy with Ruby and we rode over.

"We all got out and Mr. Stevenson hitched the horses out by the lane. He walked around the place a bit asking me some questions about how Jenny lived, and where she spent most of her time. Then, he found what he called a likely spot under the big live oak by the house and brought some little stools from the buggy for us to sit on. Took a bit of doing to get them just right before we made a little circle. He told us to hold hands and close our eyes. 'Sposed to be, if anyone made a contact, or got a spirit message, the energy flow around the circle would warn all of us to be open to the spirit. I still wasn't comfortable with it. It was sort of scary, but out in broad daylight I didn't see no harm.

"We sat there in this circle while he droned on in a mysterious voice about help and condemnation and being lost and sympathy, and I don't know what all. He kept saying, 'Empty your minds, ladies. Let the spirits guide you. I was getting exasperated trying to figure out how to empty my mind. Seemed like every thought I ever thought and some I was saving for Christmas wanted to be considered. I opened my eyes to see if the others were having any trouble. They seemed right peaceful sitting there with the shadows playin' on them. I kinda looked around toward the cabin door—and there she was. There stood Jenny, watching *us*.

"I couldn't see her just real plain. I mean, it would be hard to say that her eyes were green, and I couldn't make out that crooked tooth she had when she smiled—come to think of it, she didn't smile at all. She had a puzzlin' expression on her face, like she wondered who we were and what we were doing.

"I looked back to see if Ruby and the Stevensons knew she was there, but they were just sitting with their eyes closed while he talked on. I looked back at Jenny. She looked real strange, and I was about to wonder if I really saw her, then she threw up her hands. You know how Jenny used to do. Like this," Sally showed them, bending her arms at the elbow and flashing her hands up about face high with the palms out.

"She used to do that when she was exasperated. When she felt like she was at the end of her rope, or like she was saying, 'What now!' She'd throw up her hands like that. I knew, then, that it was Jenny for sure. I've seen her make that gesture many times. Now, she threw up her hands like that and walked off toward the creek. I started to say something to the others and looked toward them, but they were still sitting with their eyes closed and he was still talking. Then when I looked back toward Jenny, she was fading fast. I could see the pecan tree through her. Before I could make up my mind, she was gone.

"I started to speak to the rescuers again, but couldn't bring myself to. They seemed so intent on helping. After a right smart, he stopped talking and they just set there for awhile. They was real disappointed and decided to pack up and go home. Didn't seem to be a proper time for spirit contact. Somehow, I couldn't bring myself to mention about Jenny watching us. They would have wondered why I didn't tell them, why the energy didn't flow through me. How would I know?" Sally asked and ended her story.

"I do declare," said Millie. "Did they really think they could talk to Jenny, you 'spose?"

"Oh, yes. I don't doubt they thought they could set the poor soul free. They seemed convinced. And Sam and me couldn't see no other motive, unless it was like mine, curiosity," said Sally.

"That's interesting, Sally. Seems to me Jenny is a pretty independent spirit. I reckon she will appear to whoever she pleases, when she pleases," said Doc.

"Yeah, I think you're right. We may see more of Jenny. That McDow Hole is pretty important to all of us," said George, who passed the place every time he came to Alexander and often got water there.

"Well, what would we talk about if it weren't for Jenny? Guess she'll be a favorite topic of conversation for years to come." Little did Doc know what a true prophecy he made.

> "Moreover, what he saw no longer filled him
> with amazement, for he remembered it all. It
> was familiar It had all happened before just
> so. hundreds of times, and he himself had
> taken part in it and known the wild madness
> of it all "
>
> —ALGERNON BLACKWOOD
> *Ancient Sorceries*

CHAPTER XIV

Home

It was strange, the sense of peace the ghost of Jenny felt as she sat on the stump by the water barrel near the cabin. It was not a happy feeling, carrying as it did such a deep yearning…an insatiable nostalgia that was more than any physical hunger she could remember. It was more painful even than the desperate hunger she had endured during the war on that used-up plantation after two different armies had staggered through eating everything from pantry and field. Searching her past for a memory that might shelter a modicum of solace, one scene that took place just prior to their leaving Georgia began to unfold.

Nathan Papworth's house was spacious, and because of its out-of-the-way location had survived the ravages of war, but not its effects. It was a big house with two stories across a front with chimneys at each end and a porch across the length of the ground floor. In an el toward the back was a big dining room and then a breezeway that divided the kitchen from the rest of the house. Four of the six bedrooms were empty now and one more soon would be, as Nathan's only surviving son Charlie and his wife Jenny prepared to leave for Texas. Nathan had asked Charlie to stay long enough to attend the final arrangements for the freeing of the plantation slaves.

Charlie's mother sat in a rocker on the porch with her doll, arranging its dress and humming as she cradled it against her shoulder while she rocked, oblivious of what was taking place. Nathan had called the ten slaves to the lawn to tell them about the arrangements.

"People, this is a sad day for me, and a sad day for the South. I don't know what is to become of you—or of us. You have many choices before you and I can only hope you will make the ones best for yourselves and each other.

"I propose to give each family a cow, a pig and a sack of corn. I wish I had money to give, but all of mine is Confederate and has no value. After talking with Jethro and Eliza and finding them willing, I will deed them ten acres of land to the east of their cabin for which they have agreed to do us a service." The grey heads of Jethro and Eliza nodded to show they were in agreement.

"Eliza has agreed to take care of the missus and to cook for us. Jethro will help me with the crops—though we'll not be doing much. After a year, I hope to be able to pay these loyal servants wages. But for now, all I can promise is to share what we have. The rest of you are free to go wherever you like. May God go with you."

It was a sad scene full of goodbyes and tears and, no doubt for the younger negroes, a measure of happiness. Jenny didn't realize how complete the change in her life style would follow this moment, but it was clear that for those who stayed behind as well as those who were leaving, some painful adjustment and sacrifice lay in wait.

"You were right, Charlie. You were so right. The sickness was the first concern, but life, as I wanted it, was gone. We couldn't stay, and we could never go home again."

The heartbreak of that scene, the aging of Nathan and Mary, the uncertainty of life, the uncompromising struggle for better days—Jenny finally knew—were not hers alone, nor were they made in Texas.

"I'm sorry, Charlie. Understanding comes so late. But I am sorry," she said to her ghostly self as she sat on the stump and viewed the familiar surroundings. *"This really is home."*

She flitted from one center of her homemaking to another, even going inside the cabin and remembering the spiders, lizards and centipedes that now seemed only part of a bigger struggle. She looked at the stools and remembered how Charlie worked by firelight until late at night, trying to bring a little comfort and joy to ease her discontent.

"You were such a dear good man, Charlie," she said as she glanced back over her shoulder. With ghostly finger she caressed the cover of the water barrel without disturbing the accumulation of blow sand. Temple had struggled to dip the bucket when the water level got low, she thought with a pang of love in her heart. *"Where is my son? Where is my Temple? I loved him so. Did he know? Will he ever come back? Surely he knows I'm waiting."*

It was sunrise on a frosty morning in October. As the pink tinge of dawn spread into the morning blue of the sky, she saw a lone figure standing under the pecan tree between the cabin and the creek. She transported her thoughts and her essence to the vicinity of the tree and recognized Doctor Jed. In the hush of the still morning she watched and waited.

"He's leaving the county, but he hates to go until he knows about me." She tried no more successfully than Doc to analyze the transfer of knowledge between them. It was enough that he knew more about her than any mortal ever had, either while she was alive or in her present state. She felt a kinship with the big man. *"He wonders why I cannot go on to my rest now that Brownlow is dead and the secret is out. It has made a difference, but something still holds me here. Am I being punished because my love was so cold when I was here in life? Is it because I failed to give enough in that life that I find no comfort in this death? Too late. It's too late to undo my trespasses. What still tears at my heart now? Hate is nearly gone. Those other gnawing human hungers are fading. Why am I here?"*

Jenny wondered about the meaning of time. Without a body for a clock, time had lost its command over her life. Hours, days, years—little could she know of their passage. She realized that since Brownlow's death there had been gaps in her sojourn, almost peaceful periods, when her spirit was not so restless.

"Yes, he'll be back, but will our paths cross? He would like to help, both because of his innate kindness and as a sort of penance for some misdeed. I can't understand. Something has changed him, made him gentle and accepting. Maybe he cared too much…as I cared too little. He has a sympathetic spirit. He's trying to say goodbye to me…and to this place, almost as if it were his. Maybe another who understands will come. Maybe I'll no longer be here. But this is home. How strange the place that felt so foreign to me when I was alive should become the place I cannot leave."

"I'll be here, Jed, should you come back. I'll be here."

Jed stood, uncertain of his reasons for taking a last look at the place where he had done so much soul searching. His efforts to understand Jenny had somehow brought awareness and acceptance of his own faults, and once accepted, filled him with a new freedom—a freedom to grow instead of continuing to erect more defenses.

"It's strange, isn't it, Jenny? Neither of us intended to call this country home. If only I could have found release from all that hate and vengeance earlier, maybe I could have shown more love to Florence. Certainly she deserved more than I gave. Still I think she knew I loved her. She knew me better than I knew myself. She even found some goodness hidden under the bluff and bluster." As he remembered, Jed frowned and rolled the brim of his hat.

"At least we grew closer after all the trouble. I suppose we began to realize just how much we really needed each other, how lonely—" he stifled a sob and rubbed his damp eyes with the back of his hand.

"Perhaps it's good that I didn't come while you were alive, Jenny. This affinity, this bond between us, might have been too much had we known each other in life. We both had other loves, other loyalties. Still, I feel like we missed something very precious."

Embarrassed by the thought, he looked toward the sunrise and said, "But we were different people then. We might not have even liked each other."

He looked toward the tree tops above the cabin to change his train of thought. "It's a glorious morning, isn't it? Time for a new beginning. But I will be coming back, for no other place holds me as this one does. I guess that's what home is, a place that seems to pull at your hopes and plans." Then he turned back around and saw Jenny, bending over to pick up pecans as she must have done many times before. She filled her hand and let the pecans drop into the woven straw basket she held.

Doc watched for a moment and then, without thinking, began to pick up pecans himself. He walked over and dropped them into Jenny's basket. He jumped back with a start when the pecans he dropped fell noisily to the ground. He could see the basket but it offered no resistance...then, to his amazement, before his eyes, both Jenny and her basket faded away.

It took Jed a few minutes to regain his composure, then shaking his head he muttered, "High time I had a vacation. Maybe I'm getting a little light headed."

He mounted his horse and rode toward the lane, looking back once to wave at the phantom standing by the tree, acknowledging that a part of himself was woven into the shimmering colors of the spirit world.

Jenny watched him go. *"I'll still be here, friend."* She knew now that she could appear and disappear as she chose, but it seemed to require more effort. Still in control she waited and wondered—would Charlie ever return? Would Temple? Would he remember her? Would she feel a kinship, a mother's love if Temple should come home? Surely love does not die as long as spirits exist. Clutching her sadness, Jenny floated to the deep water of the McDow Hole and hovered there for a few minutes before she disappeared.

EPILOGUE

Jenny's Helpers

I t's a funny world, ain't it, Hi? Here everybody is trying to explain away Jenny's ghost and still making kids believe in Santa Claus," said Will.

"What do you mean, Will?"

"Seems to me if we can believe in them stories about sleeping beauties that wake up after hundreds of years, we have a right to believe in ghosts. Like some poor stubborn cuss that only wants to walk around a mite after he's dead and buried," explained Will.

Will and Hi were taking a breather from unloading bales of hay from a wagon into the barn. They straightened their tired backs and leaned against a large stack of bales. Both young men were crowding eighteen and lived on adjoining farms. When harvesting time came, or hay hauling time, they helped each other so they could enjoy their free time together. Besides, their fathers believed in keeping them busy to keep them out of mischief. Between the two of them, they could think of many ways to court trouble in spite of what their parents wanted.

Hi was tall and skinny; in fact, he was called "High Pockets" because his pockets were so high from his big feet, but most people just called him "Hi." He always wore gloves when he worked in the field because he played the fiddle and wanted to keep his fingers sensitive to the strings. His blue eyes got all dreamy when he tucked the fiddle under his long, cleft chin and pulled music from the air. Will, on the other hand, was box-shaped, square, not fat, but heavy and muscular from such tasks as loading hay and walking miles and miles hanging to a plow behind Ole Babe, one of the farm mules. He lifted his old beat-up hat and rubbed his thatch of curly dark brown hair.

"Yeah, it's strange. Cows jump over the moon when you are four or five, but ghosts cain't walk on water when you get to about fourteen. Seems to me the preacher said t'other Sunday that a woman named Rhoda in the Bible once thought she saw a ghost," said Hi, chewing on a piece of hay and reaching down to pet the calico cat that rubbed against his legs. He liked all kinds of animals and they seemed to pick him out of a crowd.

"Now Jenny—there was a ghost with a vengeance! Anyone that came in her territory was in danger of being terrified. Remember that yankee feller that didn't believe in ghosts and tried to stay the night in her cabin? Next morning he was long gone. No one ever saw him here 'bouts again."

"Wonder how she looked to him? Some say she just sorta materialized out over the water. You'd see nothing at first, then she'd form out of smoke or fog. She usually had that baby in her arms," mused Hi.

"Yeah, after old man Brownlow admitted on his death bed that he killed her and the baby, looks like she would rest in peace," said Will.

"Hey, you talk like you really believe she was there!"

"Why are you saying WAS? Ain't she still around?"

"I think she's gone. People keep trying to explain her away. They say a warm spring bubbling up through the other water in that hole on Green's Creek caused the fog that looked like a ghost. And a screech owl that used to roost in the big pecan tree got tired of being disturbed and moved his headquarters. Raccoons made all the noise around the cabin, I guess. I reckon she lost her grip and went — wherever ghosts and fairies and elves go," Hi said.

"Well, if Jenny's not around, who's going to take care of the scaring when the high school kids have that picnic supper down at the ghost hole this weekend?" asked Will.

"Come to think on it, seems like a real shame, them going down there expecting to be scared half to death and Jenny not around." Hi felt a plan coming on.

"Yeah, maybe we ought to give Jenny a little help, encourage her maybe."

"Yeah, that'd be more fun than when we put that lizard in the teacher's purse." Hi had a twinkle in his eyes as he thought of the possibilities.

So the planning began. Jenny's helpers decided that the high schoolers needed something to write about. They could just imagine all those papers beginning, "The time I saw the ghost of Jenny."

Will borrowed one of his mother's old dresses, a light, faded blue one that would look white in the moonlight. He wished he could use her new white one, but realized his life would be worth little if anything happened to it. They hitched a pulley from the big pecan tree, the hanging tree some called it, though it was too close to the water to be that one, to a stump on the other side of the creek.

"We better not put the dress on the pulley until after sundown. Someone might come by early and see it," said Hi.

"You're right. We better not give cause for suspicion."

Everything had to be planned just right. Chances were, when the picnic party ate their supper around the campfire, they would begin to tell ghost stories. That's the way such parties usually progressed. Will and Hi would have all the props ready, and be watching for that time.

The east bank of the Ghost Hole, where the big pecan tree reached out to shade the water in the daytime, was high, about five feet above the water. Other smaller pecan trees struggled to find sun and soil enough to grow nearby. The west bank sloped down to the water leaving a gravel shoal which gave way to pasture grass above the bank. Both sides were brushy, except for the gravelly part and clearings trampled down by cows coming to water on the low side, with briars, sumac, scrub willows and tall weeds.

Autumn was show time for the color display. Red sumac clung to the bottom of the hill and straggled down to join wild thicket plums changing to the lighter green of willows near the creek bank. Mustang grapes clinging to oak and pecan swiped the scene with a deeper green. The winey smell of overripe grapes rose teasingly from the undergrowth. In the daylight the clear water of the creek looked like a good place to fish for goggle-eyed perch and channel catfish, but at night the scene became eerie, other-worldly.

Will and Hi rode their horses over to a lane just over the hill from the east bank. They went early to have plenty of time to make sure all their props were in place and that the pulley worked. Hi brought his fiddle. He had been practicing all afternoon, making screaming, screeching noises that sounded ghost-like, he hoped. After checking things they rode on over to Alexander to wait until dark.

Arriving when the red and golden glow of the sunset was just beginning to fade, the twelve students jumped out of the back of the teacher's 1930 International truck. Soon they had their supplies unloaded and a fire blazing to ward off darkness. They were full of chatter and laughter, jostling, chasing, teasing in the fading day, until their noise and merriment was dampened by encroaching night. Soon it was quiet enough for them to hear the crackling of the fire, the stirring of the weeds and grass when an occasional breeze dipped down over the rim of the hill to follow the creek. Shadows cast by the firelight began to play on the water, and the limbs of the pecan tree reaching for them seemed threatening but— enticing.

A mourning dove called plaintively from further down the creek, "Follow me, come, come. Follow me, come, come." Soon a mate was answering from a willow just beyond the picnic site, "Follow me, come," making a woeful conversation that stopped the talk around the campfire for a few minutes.

Eyes searched and ears strained, "It's just doves," said one brave soul. "My grandpa said there was no mistaking Jenny for an owl or anything natural. When she screams she shatters everything within earshot."

Across the creek on the high bank, Will was fastening the dress to the pulley and Hi was stationed behind the trunk of the tree with fiddle in hand. Both were watching the party across the creek—near enough to hear the talking, but too far away to understand the words being spoken quietly as the twelve huddled closer together near the fire. The ghost helpers waited as time ripened. The movements against the dancing flames cast gyrating shadows on the water for Will and Hi to watch. The unreal shadow world was nearer than the real world identified by odors of home-cured ham slices roasting on sticks, and coffee boiling. The mourning doves, identified but unseen, became more sorrowful as their calls began to dominate the night noises.

Will and Hi began to feel that maybe Jenny didn't understand their purpose! They could feel her presence and interest in them, but it didn't feel too friendly! Will had chill bumps of fear on his neck and shoulders, but they were determined that nothing could deter them from their task. Will was just about to say, "Ready?" when a woman rose from the water at the head of the water hole. Her filmy white dress floated just above the surface of the water as she glided into plain sight. She was coming down the creek, walking on the water! That was no vapor! That was no fog! That was a woman in a white dress just below the banks where Will and Hi stood transfixed. She was coming right at them.

When she got close to them, Jenny—it had to be her—turned her head to stare directly at them with eyes like coals of fire. They could see the withered skin of her mummy-like face. Then she screamed! A piercing, harrowing, quivering scream whose echoes bounced from every rock, branch, tree, briar and weed in the area.

Will and Hi didn't wait for the second act, but began to scramble through the briars which grabbed with ghostly fingers to rip shirts and scratch skin. Hi, tangled in a mustang grape vine, fell into a ravine. The fiddle went "Twing," and then "Twang," as his knee and then his big foot smashed it, but he didn't stop to reckon the damage. Lurching to his feet he called, "Wait for me, Will! Wait for me."

Across the creek young people trampled food, quilts, fire and each other as they made a mad scramble for the truck. The motor roared into life as the school party made for the road, looking back over shoulders with eyes stretched wide open. Supplies would have to wait to be found in the daylight.

Will and Hi didn't stop until they reached their horses, both of whom picked up their owners' fright and began to neigh and paw as the young men mounted and headed for home.

After a few minutes, when both of them had a chance to catch their breath, Will said, "It 'pears as how Jenny don't need nobody's help, Hi!"